Persecution
in the Early Church

by

HERBERT B. WORKMAN

with a Foreword by
Michael Bourdeaux

D1484822

Oxford New York Toronto Melbourne
OXFORD UNIVERSITY PRESS
1980

Oxford University Press, Walton Street, Oxford OX2 6DP

OXFORD LONDON GLASGOW
NEW YORK TORONTO MELBOURNE WELLINGTON
KUALA LUMPUR SINGAPORE JAKARTA HONG KONG TOKYO
DELHI BOMBAY CALCUTTA MADRAS KARACHI
NAIROBI DAR ES SALAAM CAPE TOWN

Original edition 1906
First paperback edition in
Wyvern Books (Epworth Press) 1960

First published as an Oxford University Press paperback 1980
Foreword © Michael Bourdeaux 1980
Bibliography © W. H. C. Frend 1980

British Library Cataloguing in Publication Data

Workman, Herbert Brook
Persecution in the Early Church
1. Persecution – Early church 0.30–600
I. Title
272'.1   BR1604.2   79–42765
ISBN 0–19–283025–2

Set, printed and bound in Great Britain by
Cox & Wyman Ltd, Reading

FOREWORD

by Michael Bourdeaux, Director of Keston College

'TODAY here, as in Pilate's day, Christ our Saviour is being judged.' With these words Georgi Vins, the Russian Baptist leader, resigned himself to what turned out to be eight years of imprisonment in sub-human conditions, broken by spells of 'liberty', during most of which he was on the run from the police. This first trial of Vins in November 1966 lasted twenty-nine hours, and was crammed into two days, ending with the sentence at 1 a.m. Its illegalities were not dissimilar in some aspects from the trial of Christ, so tellingly analysed by Dr. Workman in the first chapter of the present book. Even the charges against Vins of breaking the laws on the separation of Church and state were a technicality designed to mask the nature of the basic 'crime': a challenge to the state on its claim to own even the minds of its subjects. Dr. Workman's analysis of the crime of *majestas* against the Roman Empire (pp. 4–9) is similar enough to justify a mention of the two in the same context.

A book which is a classic will demonstrate itself as being relevant to any age. *Persecution in the Early Church* is certainly in this category, yet even the intuitions of the author may not have granted him the perception that his book would have been more relevant to the world of today than to that of 1906 when he finished it. No decade this century needs a republication of this book more than the 1980's, and this for a variety of reasons.

As we look back over the last sixty years of Church history a perspective begins to emerge. One of its component features is an unbroken sequence of persecution: the Soviet Union under Lenin and Stalin; Germany under Hitler; Czechoslovakia, the Baltic States, Poland, and elsewhere under Stalin again; the U.S.S.R. later under Khrushchev; Albania under Chinese hegemony; China itself under Mao; Uganda under Amin; Cambodia under Pol Pot. The list is growing. A persecuted Church needs moral support from the Early Church. Those not persecuted must be inspired to help those who are. The present book is the best popular account of the facts. In its first edition it contained a heavy armoury of critical apparatus. Shorn of this, it was republished by the Epworth Press in 1960. The text itself stood entirely on its own feet and can do so again, though this time there is a Select Bibliography compiled by Professor W. H. C. Frend.

The publishers are correct in their decision not to update or edit the original text in any way. Modern research has revealed little necessitating any basic modification of what Dr. Workman wrote. His occasional references to the late-Victorian world in which he did his research may give it a period flavour, yet they demonstrate his perception and, in a way, are curiously prophetic. They are mainly to that land which was soon to witness the worst-ever persecution of the faith: 'Just as in modern Russia the Nihilist or the innocent reformer can be arrested or sentenced, even banished for life to Sakhalien, on mere "administrative order", without the pretence of trial, or the need that the bureaucrat quote any law at all, so with the early Christian' (p. 25). Even Russian anti-semitism is condemned on p. 43.

The informed reader will shudder at the pages (81ff) where the author discusses the total number of Christian martyrs in the age of the Early Church. He is indeed very slightly critical of Jerome, hyperbolical though the latter's computation was clearly intended to be, when he wrote: 'There is no day in the whole year into which the number of five thousand martyrs cannot be ascribed, except only the first day of January' (p. 81).

Well, $5,000 \times 364 = 1,820,000$! The documentary records for scaling down (or indeed confirming) Jerome's figure are absent from the pages of history. So are they from contemporary annals – incredibly in an age so enamoured of statistics on economic growth and the world population. Yet bold would be the man who claimed that fewer than two million Christians have given up their life for the faith in this century. We are talking of sixty years; Dr. Workman's span was four times as long. Jerome's figure could well be exceeded by the martyrs of Stalin's Russia alone. Yet their story is perhaps more enshrouded in the mists of the unknown than that of those recounted here. Perhaps this republication may stimulate a first assessment of the martyr witness of the twentieth century, towards which a start has been made by Diana Dewar in the book *All for Christ* mentioned on the cover of this book.

Anonymous millions are overwhelmed by waves of persecution, about which only the occasional name, only the occasional deed, claims individual attention. The interval between the crests of those waves has been less this century than in the Early Church (p. 82), the causes of persecution more diversified, the possibility of finding sanctuary less in an age where totalitarianism is backed by technology. The catacombs of Rome (p. 103f.) may have a certain inviolability; those into which the Church of the 1930's in the Soviet Union was driven had none. The resultant sufferings were in no way less. The present generation of the faithful in our self-indulgent society is infinitely the poorer spiritually for failing to draw inspiration from elsewhere in the world today. Even more it needs to look back to its origins in the Roman world of eighteen centuries ago.

I read this book while on a visit to Poland. The resonance of Dr. Workman's text deepened the diapason of the experience. In Warsaw today the Church does physically provide sanctuary for hunger-strikers demonstrating for human rights, and the police are afraid to touch them when they are thus protected. More significant is the universal dedication to a Church which has been refined by persecution. The carbon under intense pressure now has the sparkle of the diamond; and it has acquired a cutting edge of evangelism as well. Ninety-five per cent of Poles practise their faith expressed through the tradition of the Roman Catholic Church. It is not by chance that this nation has provided Pope John Paul II, whose words and deeds inspire the world.

Persecution can, of course, also root out religion where it is weak in quality (p. 142). Perhaps it has in Albania; more likely such a sweeping statement will soon be proved wrong, as it already has been of China, where, in some form, the faith is re-emerging. Wherever it does, it proves the tremendous words of Tertullian, with which Dr. Workman concludes his study, that 'the blood of the martyrs is indeed the seed of the Church'.

CONTENTS

Chapter One

THE MASTER AND HIS DISCIPLES

I

In the history of the Christian Church the student is brought face to face at the very outset with the extremist forms that renunciation can take. No scale has yet been devised that can weigh the relative value of different methods of self-surrender. That which is ease and simplicity to one man may be the needle's eye to another; the source of exquisite pain for one may be for his fellow a matter of little consequence. The outsider who would construct a table of renunciatory values is face to face with the same difficulty which besets any utilitarian theory of morals, that pain and pleasure are absolutely relative terms. However this may be, in one thing most men are agreed: that the voluntary surrender of life itself represents the highest renunciation. 'Skin for skin, yea all that a man hath will he give for his life,' is still true, in spite of the efforts of Schopenhauer and others to demonstrate its illogical character.

The consciousness of the Christian Church has decided the question. In all ages men have looked upon the martyr as the highest expression of the spirit of self-surrender; in every country and century he has won for himself that homage and esteem which renunciation, whether in greater or less degree, never fails to procure. 'Blessed Martyrs,' wrote one, long ago, 'ye who have been tried by fire like fine gold, ye are now crowned with the diadem that cannot fade away; for ye have bruised beneath your feet the serpent's head.'

The consciousness of the Christian Church cannot be seriously questioned. There are cases, it is true, in which it is easier to die than to live; where the daily discharge of duty against overwhelming odds, the daily carrying of a burden that only death can remove, the daily suppression of a pain that is gnawing the heart, the daily struggle of broken wings against the prison bars, is a task far more difficult than one heroic rush into the midst of the foe, one short hour of pain, and then kindly peace for ever. The time-factor, in a word, cannot be ignored; and probably if the amount of pain could be calculated, there are saints all around us the sum of whose sufferings drawn out through years outweighs the brief tortures that have immortalized the noble army of martyrs. But this time-factor is one that in practical life it is generally impossible to estimate. The Victoria Crosses are for the heroes of the moment; there are no rewards for the lifelong sufferers that war brings in her train. So also in the Christian Church. The valuation of the time-factor must be left with God; we have no instruments where with we can measure it. But one thing the dullest can understand – the worth and reality of the renunciation and self-sacrifice which count life itself of no value, and which have obtained, in the fine figure of Tertullian, 'the crown of eternity itself.'

In part, no doubt, the value that the Christian Church has always attached to martyrdom must be attributed to the example of Jesus, if for the moment we may contemplate the Crucifixion not in its eternal significance as atonement, but under its aspect as an episode in human history. The story that moved the world was the Cross. *In hoc signo vinces* may be a legend of later growth; none the less it was a historical fact. A crossless Saviour would be a crownless king; for Christ the 'hour' of His crucifixion was the 'hour' of His glory, the one 'hour' of His timeless being. For Him also was fulfilled the saying 'The crown blossoms on thorns.' In spite of the sneers of Lucian at the 'crucified Sophist,' the Martyr of Calvary laid His spell on the world from the first; a fact the more remarkable when we remember that mere suffering could never have appealed to an age that was steeped in cruelty, and for whom crucifixion, the punishment of slaves, was one of the commonest sights of life. Through His cross the Man of Sorrows became the crowned King, 'whose pierced hand lifted empires off their hinges, and turned the stream of centuries out of its channel, and still governs the ages.' The spear that pierced His side was in reality the death-wound of the old paganism. 'Pan, great Pan is dead,' is one of the undertones in the cry of triumph, 'It is finished.' Very beautifully is this expressed in a recent poem:

> Girt in the panther fells,
>   Violets in my hair,
> Down I ran through the woody dells,
>   Through the morning wild and fair,—
> To sit by the road till the sun was high,
> That I might see some god pass by.
>
> Fluting amidst the thyme
>   I dreamed through the golden day,
> Calling through melody and rhyme,
>   'Iacchus! come this way,—
> From harrowing Hades like a king,
> Vine leaves and glorious scattering.'

Twilight was all rose-red
　　When, crowned with vine and thorn,
Came a stranger-god from out the dead;
　　And his hands and feet were torn.
I knew him not, for he came alone:
I knew him not, when I fain had known.

He said: 'For love, for love
　　I wear the vine and thorn.'
He said: 'For love, for love
　　My hands and feet were torn:
For love the wine-press Death I trod.'
And I cried in pain: 'O Lord my God.'

The Cross is the peculiar property of the Gospel. 'None of the so-called sons of Jupiter did imitate the being crucified,' argued Justin; the idea was as new in the thought of the world as its power was tremendous. 'The old logicians,' writes Dr. Bigg, 'used to say that everything should be defined *per genus et differentiam*. Christianity is a religion; this is its *genus*, this it has in common with all other religions. It is the religion of vicarious sacrifice, or of the Cross, this is its *differentia*; in this addition lies the peculiar nature which makes it what it is, and distinguishes it from every other member of the same class.' The popular verdict is one with that of theological science. Theories of the Atonement have been devised more or less satisfactorily in their efforts to explain in finite symbols the infinite love and sorrow that lie at the heart of God. But even those for whom such theories are meaningless have rarely failed to render homage to the Divine Sufferer.

The speculative consequences of this position that Christianity is essentially the religion of the Cross are very great. Doctrines shared by Christianity with other religions, the beliefs in immortality and Providence, the value of law and virtue, necessarily become of secondary importance as explanatory causes of its success. This can be adequately accounted for only by that one feature in which Christianity differs from all religions that have gone before or which have risen since. The foundations of the Church are laid deep in Calvary.

Of equal importance are the practical consequences. If the Cross is the essence of Christianity, cross-bearing is the mark of every disciple of Jesus. The theology of an early disciple could scarcely fail to be otherwise than loose. Only slowly, under the pressure of circumstances, did the great doctrines become clear-cut in the consciousness of the Church. But immature as might be the current ideas on the Trinity, the Person of Christ, the nature of the Atonement, and the Personality of the Holy Ghost, on one matter there could be no hesitation or uncertainty. Jesus

Himself had said it; no man could be His disciple who should not bear
His Cross. Self-denial, renunciation, martyrdom, the 'emptying one's
self' for others, in a word, the Cross in one form or another, not for the
sake of 'my soul' merely, but for the sake of 'my brother's soul' as well as
mine, – this was the mark by which the Shepherd would know His
sheep. Alas! for that soul in whom the Master, when He came, could not
find the print of the nails, and the wounds of His passion. Self-surrender,
self-sacrifice, is not the *bene esse*, but the very *esse* of Christianity. 'The
old Gnostics called the Cross Horos, the Boundary or Dividing Line. The
Gnostics were a curious people, but they were right here.' The Cross is
indeed the dividing line, both in the life of the world, of every individual, and of the Christ Himself.

There is a beautiful story in that charming work of Sulpicius Severus,
the *Life of St Martin of Tours*, which will serve as an illustration of our
meaning. One day as Martin was praying there stood before him in his
cell a radiant being, 'clothed upon with a kingly vest, with a diadem of
gems and gold upon his brow, shoes inlaid with gold upon his feet, and
whose face was lit with joy.' As the saint stood in silence, 'Martin,' said
the vision, 'dost thou not know whom thou beholdest? I am the Christ.'
But Martin still stood erect and speechless. 'Martin,' the voice repeated,
'why dost thou doubt that thou beholdest Me? I am the Christ.' 'Not so,'
replied the saint, 'Jesus our Lord never said that He would come again
resplendent in purple and gold. I will not believe that I have seen any
vision of Christ, except He come clothed upon with the form in which
He suffered, and bearing the marks of His Cross.' At once the vision
vanished, and by the fumes with which his cell was filled Martin recognized that it had been the devil. Martin's insight was correct; the Cross
is the true mark of the Lord. Even the triumphant Christ must still
wear 'the dear tokens of His passion.'

II

At this point it will be convenient to examine the nature of the charge
and the legality of the trial by which our Lord was condemned. The
matter is of importance, not merely in itself, but by reason of its relation
to our theme. For, as we shall see, in His trial and execution our Lord
was the first-born of many brethren, condemned on essentially the same
charge and at the same court as the majority of the early Christians. But
in one detail the case of our Saviour was unique. The two most
influential law systems of the old world, the venerable law of Moses and
the august jurisprudence of Rome, had both to face the problem, 'What
shall we do with Jesus that is called the Christ?' To accomplish His

destruction they were both violently wrested into injustice, to meet the greed and allay the fears of those charged with their administration.

So long as our Lord was in Galilee the Sanhedrim had no legal authority over Him. But once in Jerusalem, He came under their control. For the Romans, wise in their generation, governed their empire by a system of devolution or modified home rule. In Judaea every effort was made to conciliate local feeling. The members of the Sanhedrim were allowed the full exercise of their judicial functions, so far as their own people were concerned, with the limitation, of importance in the case of St. Paul, that they had no control over Roman citizens, nor had they any right of inflicting the death sentence. But this last was really a less effective check than it might appear. A politic procurator, ever anxious to prevent disturbance in his province, usually ratified the death sentence of the Sanhedrim.

The arrest of Jesus on the warrant of the Sanhedrim, perhaps on the charge of riot in the Temple, was therefore legal. So assured were the high-priests of their rights that they obtained from Pilate a cohort of soldiers under a tribune to protect them in their enterprise, and to assist the Temple police. The large military force may seem excessive; evidently the hierarchy expected an outbreak of the Galileans, who neither recognized nor were accustomed to their jurisdiction. Of more importance is it to note in this persecution of the Son of Man that feature, so marked in later days, of the union of Jew and Roman. In Judaea, as afterwards throughout the world, the civil and ecclesiastical authorities were one in their effort to destroy the religion of Jesus. The actual arrest in the garden of Gethsemane seems to have been the work of the Roman soldiers, the Temple police at the critical moment yielding to a panic. They had often heard the Saviour speak; they had seen His deeds; they dreaded His power. From all these fears the more ignorant Roman soldiers were free. But with the handing over of their captive to the officers of the Sanhedrim the work of the regulars for the present was finished.

The private examination of Jesus before Annas was altogether illegal. In Judaea, unlike France or Scotland, no preliminary interrogatories were allowed. The trial before the Sanhedrim would have been legal if the court had been a formal meeting, and not a packed quorum of twenty-three, to say nothing of the doubt whether the day was not one on which all courts were illegal. As it was, its conduct made it a judicial murder. Contrary to all the rules of Jewish law, the court was held, in part at least, by night, or at any rate before daybreak. According to St Luke, the formal decision – for no witnesses were recalled – was not given until dawn. But even then it would have been illegal. Jewish law laid great stress on the necessary adjournment, over twelve hours at least, before the sentence of condemnation. The judicial use of the confession of the accused, even after solemn adjuration, was expressly forbidden. In this too Jesus was one with His brethren, who were condemned on their confession alone. Again, as Salvador tells us, 'the least discordance between the evidence of the witnesses was held to destroy its value.' The sentence itself, strictly speaking, was *ultra vires*, though too much must not be made of what in practice was often rather a technicality than otherwise. But the carrying out of the death-sentence without the consent of Pilate was difficult and dangerous, as Annas, the father-in-law of Caiaphas, knew to his cost, and as his son Annas was afterwards to learn. Annas, the father, had lost his office some thirteen years before for this very reason; and Pilate was not a procurator given to humouring the Jewish pretensions. The priests had no option, therefore, but to obtain the Roman endorsement. As a rule this would have been granted, with little, if any, inquiry. But, whether by blunder or design, in bringing the case before Pilate they changed the charge from blasphemy to treason. If they had alleged the first only, the count upon which Jesus had been condemned by the Sanhedrim, Pilate might have ratified their sentence offhand, as a matter merely of Jewish religion or politics. But in that case the death would have been by stoning, as ordained by the Jewish law, not the death on the Cross of malefactors and slaves, the only death which would overwhelm with ridicule His Messianic pretensions.

The charge of treason threw upon Pilate the necessity of a formal trial, of hearing the case *de novo* without reference to the examination of the Sanhedrim. *Crimen laesae majestatis (lése-majesté)*, or high treason against the Emperor, was the most grievous offence known to Roman law, theoretically second to sacrilege, but in reality one with it. In earlier days *majestas*, as the offence was usually called, embraced any 'crime against the Roman people, or their security' – we quote the comprehensive definition of the great Roman jurist Ulpian, as, for instance, conspiracy, the giving aid to enemies, or the aiming at the abolished office of king. With the fall of the Republic, and the accumulation in the person of a sacred Emperor of all the offices of the State, the law of *majestas* became the most potent instrument of tyranny, as vague as it was comprehensive. Any disrespect to the Emperor or his statue, even spoken words without acts, brought the offender under its penal clauses. The refusal to pay the taxes or tribute to Caesar might also, by a lawyer's ingenuity, be brought under the same head. The penalties were fixed by law as either banishment or death. How hardly all this bore on the Christians we shall see later.

On their first bringing the prisoner before Pilate the Sanhedrim attempted to obtain His condemnation on a general unspecified warrant. But when Pilate refused to touch such a case they were driven to formulate a specific accusation. By Roman law and usage each count in an indictment had to be tried separately. Of the three counts alleged against Jesus – perverting the nation, the forbidding tribute to Caesar, and the making Himself a king – Pilate fastened upon the last as the most important and comprehensive. The fact, if true, would be fatal. As procurator or imperial legate he was bound to conduct such a case himself. The trial took place in the Praetorium – either some hall in the Castle of Antonia, or, more probably, the Palace of Herod the Great – and would appear to have been but brief. In answer to the formal charge our Lord put in a plea known to English law as *confession and avoidance*, admitting in effect the truth of the accusation, but pleading 'new matter to avoid the effect of it, and show that the plaintiff is, notwithstanding, not entitled to his action.' My kingdom,' He said, 'is not of this world'. He pleaded that His kingdom dealt with spiritual things, as, for instance, the truth. After some discussion, not unmixed with scorn, Pilate accepted the plea. Evidently Jesus was a religious enthusiast, or wandering philosopher whom it would be absurd to destroy by so imposing a legal process. Let the Jews deal with the matter themselves. So far as *majestas* was concerned, Pilate pronounced the sentence of acquittal – 'I find no crime in Him', *absolvo*, Not guilty.

Up to this point Pilate had kept true to the immortal traditions of Roman equity, which more than aught else constituted the secret and strength of the Empire. But the sentence of acquittal led to an outburst of the mob, which seems to have swept Pilate off his feet. Hearing the word Galilee, he tried to change the venue, to send the prisoner from the place of arrest to the place of His crime; a step which would have been perfectly legal if only taken earlier, but which after acquittal became a travesty of justice. But Herod Antipas was too prudent to meddle in a charge of *majestas*. He turned the matter into a pleasant pantomime by arraying Jesus in 'gorgeous apparel' – either the purple robe of a king, or the white garment of a candidate – and sent Him back to Pilate. 'The Idumaean fox dreaded the lion's paw while very willing to exchange courtesies with the lion's deputy.' The after proceedings were a still deeper mockery of Roman justice; 'a veritable phantasmagoria of injustice and brutality to the accused, of alternate conciliation and expostulation towards the prosecutors, ending in the defeat of the Judge.' For two hours Pilate faced the mob, trying to accomplish the impossible – the reconciliation of acquittal and condemnation, of popularity and duty, of Roman law and Jewish fanaticism. His wife even came to the assistance of her husband's conscience. But all was in vain. At length Pilate yielded. Roman judges, pronouncing the death-sentence, called the sun to witness the justice of their acts; Pilate paid some homage to his conscience and the majesty of Roman law by taking refuge in a merely Jewish practice. He called for water, and threw the responsibility of his verdict on the priests and elders. Mob rule and priestly hatred had conquered. Utilitarian theories of justice and politics had won their greatest triumph. Christ was at length informally condemned on the charge of *majestas*, in spite of His previous judicial acquittal. In years to come, when facing the mob of Lyons, Smyrna, or Antioch on the same charge, and with the same issue as their Master, the Christians would comfort themselves with the thought that they were treading in His steps. In this, as in all else, He was their forerunner and example.

In His punishment also Christ suffered with His brethren. They were tortured as part of their examination. From this the lingering remnants of justice in Pilate's mind had spared Him, though the mockeries of Herod's soldiers were not without elements of brutality. But after the informal verdict He drank the cup to the dregs. He was bound to the whipping-post and lashed with leather thongs loaded with balls of lead or spikes of bone; then handed over to the soldiers to furnish a half-hour's jest in the barrack-room. Naturally the sport took its colour from the legal proceedings. The declared rival of Caesar should enter His kingdom. So the soldiers clothed Him with purple, some worn-out garment of Pilate, then crowned Him with thorns, and kept marching round Him, pretending to kneel as they passed. According to one authority, Pilate even sank so low as to join in their sport, characteristically combining with his undignified brutality a last effort at release. But all was in vain. The Jews pointed out that there were other counts in the indictment with which Pilate had not dealt, even if he were disposed to pay no further heed to the charge of treason, on which, in fact, he had already pronounced informal condemnation, and which they for their part were inclined to press, if necessary, by appeal to Rome. Pilate was entangled in the meshes of his own weakness. To let off a prisoner whom he had already condemned, however informally, for *majestas*, would be too dangerous for him to contemplate. There was no help for it but to pronounce the formal sentence. So Pilate ascended his tribunal, an elevated seat on a mosaic pavement, commanding, it would seem, a view over the whole city. In accordance with Roman forms, the public was admitted, and the prisoner brought in, still wearing His robes and crown. The verdict was read. As the superscription on His cross shows, Jesus was condemned for *majestas*. The death penalty was inevitable, nor was it more cruel than the penalties in England, until recent days, for the same offence. The due forms would be observed. *'Illum duci ad crucem placet,'* said the Judge, to the prisoner. *'I miles, expedi crucem,'* 'Go, soldier, get ready the cross,' he would add as he bade the officials execute the sentence without delay. With the writing of the official *titulus*, a board giving the crime, usually carried before the prisoner, and the forwarding a précis of the case to Rome, or at least entering it in the archives at Jerusalem or Caesarea, Pilate's task was finished. So the Man of Sorrows passed out to His death, carrying as usual His own cross – not the cross rendered familiar by the exaggerations of artists, for the Romans wasted no wood on their criminals. In one sense the charge of *majestas* on the 'title' was true. The King had come to His own at last. Lifted up in shame, He drew all men to Him in adoration.

III

By a sure instinct the Church discerned in the death of the martyr the repetition, not the less real because faint, of the central Sacrifice of Calvary. 'As we behold the martyrs,' writes Origen, 'coming forth from every Church to be brought before the tribunal, we see in each the Lord Himself condemned.' So Irenaeus speaks of the martyrs as 'endeavouring to follow in the footsteps of Christ', and of St. Stephen, as 'imitating in all things the Master of Martyrdom'. In the early Church the imitation of Christ, as a formal principle in ethics, played but a secondary part, so far, at any rate, as the average member was concerned. The martyrs and confessors alone were thought of as actually following and imitating Jesus; they were pre-eminently the 'true disciples' of the Master. It was enough for the servant that he should be as his Lord.

One consequence of this last idea made its appearance in the Church at a very early date. We refer to the legends of martyrdom of the first Apostles. These are manifestly the production of an age which could scarcely conceive of a perfect renunciation which did not issue in the cross or the stake. Such Christians interpreted too literally the cry of love: Let us also go, that we may die with Him. They reduced the way of the cross to one well-trodden path. They remembered, perhaps too literally, our Lord's ordination charge to His disciples, with its foreshadowings of the hour when they should stand before kings and governors for His name's sake, and its warning of the greater fear that the fear of them that kill the body and after that have no more that they can do. We in these latter days, for whom self-surrender must take a different form, not the less complete because of gentler type, may rejoice that God's demands upon His servants are not all the same. They also serve who stand and wait, and the Apostles who died in peace at home are not less truly His heroes than they who, like St. Paul or St. Peter, counted their lives to be but dross for the sake of Christ.

These legends, moreover, must be discredited, inasmuch as they are largely the outcome of the parousian beliefs which dominated the early Church. We see in them the attempts to show that the Gospel had been preached to every nation, even by the first Apostles, and that all things, therefore, were ready for His coming. But the absence of early tradition is almost proof of their falsity; at any rate, we are not now able to distinguish the kernel of fact which the legends, many of them of Gnostic or Ebionite origin, may contain.

Slight, however, as may be their basis of fact, the student would do well to remember the wise words of Dr. Montague James:

> Not many will deny that these books possess considerable historical value. The high-road will serve us well if we want to visit our cathedral cities; but in order to get an idea of the popular architecture of a district we must often digress into obscure and devious by-paths. The apocryphal books stand in the relation of by-paths – not always clean or pleasant – to the broad and well-trodden high-road of ordinary patristic literature. If a future historian wants to realize vividly what were the beliefs of many large classes of ordinary Christians in our time, he will derive great help, I doubt not, from the 'Sunday Stories' of the last thirty years: and not less information can be gathered from the apocryphal books as to the popular beliefs of average Christians in far earlier times.

The same remark is equally true of many of the less authentic Acts of Martyrs.

The record of the earliest martyr, Stephen, is in the Scriptures. In his case the lead in prosecution would appear to have been taken by the synagogue of the Roman freedmen, possibly through the influence of another Roman citizen, a young man from Tarsus, a most bitter enemy of the new Way. Immediately after the stoning of the proto-martyr a general persecution, which reached as far as Damascus, drove all except the Apostles from the city. By what means the twelve were able to stay on and yet escape destruction we know not.

From the Acts also we learn how Herod Agrippa I, the grandson of Herod, killed James, the brother of John, with the sword, and would have seized St. Peter, whose time, however, was not yet come. According to Clement of Alexandria, the man who had led St. James to the judgement-seat, possibly, though not necessarily, his accuser, was so impressed with his testimony that he too professed faith in Christ, the first of many led to the truth by the 'witness' of the 'martyrs'. Both therefore were led away to die. On their way he entreated James to be forgiven by him. James, considering a little while, replied, "Peace be to thee," and kissed him. So these two were beheaded together.' Thus St James drank at last of the same cup, and was baptized with the baptism of Christ.

> O great Apostle! rightly now
> Thou readest all thy Saviour meant.

With St. James there seems to have perished a disciple of our Lord belonging to the highest caste in the hierarchy, who bore the somewhat common name of John. Possibly this mysterious martyr suffered later, perhaps at the same time as the other St. James. But the date, the place of execution, and the identity of this John are alike matters of dispute. Some have boldly claimed that this early martyr was the Apostle John, i.e. John the son of Zebedee; others have recognized in him the shadowy 'Elder John' of Papias; not a few have denied his existence. Unfortunately the solution of the question is so wrapped up with the most momentous issues of New Testament criticism that it has become the favourite battle-ground of opposing schools.

Of the martyrdom of the other James, the brother of our Lord, the first Bishop of Jerusalem, we have an account in Hegesippus, the exact historical value of which it is difficult for the historian to appraise. But though the details may be doubtful, some of them evidently written for polemical ends, we may accept, though not without misgivings, the truth of the main outlines. By the strictness of his life and his exceeding piety – 'his knees had become as hard as camels' in consequence of his habitual supplication' – St. James had won the respect of all parties. So the rulers came to James and said, 'We entreat thee restrain the people who are led astray after Jesus ... for we all have confidence in thee. Persuade them not to be led astray. Stand therefore upon a wing of the Temple that thy words may be heard by all the people.' Then they placed James upon a wing of the Temple and cried out to him, 'O thou Just One, since the people are led astray after Jesus who was crucified, declare to us what is the door to Jesus the crucified.' But James announced with a loud voice, 'Why do ye ask me respecting Jesus the Son of Man? He is now sitting in the heavens, on the right hand of a great Power, and is about to come on the clouds of heaven.' In their rage at his testimony they hurled him down from the tower and stoned him. But he kneeled down and prayed: 'I entreat Thee God and Father forgive them, for they know not what they do.' 'Stop your stoning,' cried one of the priests, 'the Just One is praying for you.' 'But a fuller ran up, and beat out his brains with the club which he used to beat his clothes.' The story may be little more than a romance; but it was a romance with a purpose. The tale was intended to show that 'in James, the Lord's brother, we have the prototype of these later saints, whose rigid life and formal devotion elicits, it may be, the contempt of the world, but of whom nevertheless, the world was not, and is not, worthy.' The death of St. James thus set the seal on the doctrine of renunciation. The cross, as Tertullian exhausts his eloquence in showing us, is the sacred legacy of all who are His, without which there could not be perfection.

The murder of St. James was the last great event of which we possess any knowledge in the long persecution of the Christians at Jerusalem. Seven years later 'those who believed in Christ' migrated to Pella, driven out by the tyranny of the Zealot party, who were now supreme in the doomed city. As we shall see later, their sufferings at the hands of the Jews did not cease with the destruction of the Temple. From the days of St. Stephen until their final extinction the Judaistic Church knew no peace, save perhaps during the brief years spent in exile. The murder of James was more than a crime; for the future both of Christianity and Judaism it was a disaster. Judaistic Christianity, the earliest form of Christianity, was doomed. Henceforth Christianity could be of but one type. But the gain of Christianity by this concentration of itself upon one line of development was purchased by the loss of that sympathetic toleration which the existence of another type would have rendered needful. Upon none did this loss of the spirit of Jesus fall more hardly in a later age than upon the Jews themselves.

A few years before their murder of James the Just the Jews tried hard to destroy the Apostle whom they considered the great enemy of their creed. St. Peter and St. John had already left Jerusalem, possibly because with growing light they felt out of touch with its rigid Judaistic Christianity, when a fortunate chance delivered, as they thought, St. Paul himself into the hands of the priests. The story of the persecution of the great Apostle is told at some length, and throws much light on the methods employed by the Jews in their attacks upon the Christians. Not that this was the first time that St. Paul had suffered at their hands. In one of his letters he refers to the imprisonments and scourgings by which the Jews had tried to destroy his Gospel. But this new persecution so manifestly formed a crisis in the life of the Apostle and the Church that St. Luke devotes special attention to it.

Some years before there had happened in Jerusalem a notable instance of lynch law. The mob, incited by the Sanhedrim, had stoned to death the most far-sighted of the Nazarenes, trusting to the weakness or indifference of the procurators to overlook this glaring defiance of order. The leader on that occasion was one Saul of Tarsus, against whom, now that occasion demanded, the same methods might be employed. A report spread that St. Paul had introduced into the Temple one of his un-circumcized converts. The rumour was cunningly devised, for the

Romans had given the Jews the power of putting to death any Gentile, even though a Roman citizen, who profaned by his presence the sacred building. The mob did not stop to investigate its truth. They fell upon the Apostle and tried to drag him out of the Temple into the court of the Gentiles, intending there to beat him to death. But a company of soldiers on duty in the neighbouring castle of Antonia, the walls of which overlooked the sacred precincts, had observed and reported the tumult. They ran down the steps, secured the cause of the disturbance, and bound St. Paul with 'two chains', i.e. with handcuffs, to a soldier on either side. On the order being given that he should be removed to the citadel an ugly rush was made by the mob. But the soldiers lifted St. Paul into their arms and carried him up the steps to the castle. At the top Lysias the tribune, who was himself with several centurions superintending the proceedings, allowed the fettered prisoner to address the people, an irregularity which in the upshot drove the mob into fresh riot. St. Paul was hurried into the castle and orders given for his examination by torture. From this he was saved by pleading his Roman citizenship. Lysias was in a difficulty. As a citizen St. Paul must be set free or some definite charge under Roman, not Jewish, law brought against him. The attempts of Lysias to conciliate the Sanhedrim, and at the same time obtain a definite charge, ended in the renewal of the riot, and the carrying off of the Apostle once more to the castle. But the Jews were determined not to be baulked of their prey. Where the mob had failed forty desperadoes might succeed. But the plot was revealed, and St. Paul despatched for safety under an armed escort to Caesarea. With St. Paul was forwarded an official statement from Lysias of the charges against him (*elogium*) 'to his excellency the procurator Felix.'

Felix, in accordance with the usual forms, registered the charge and sent at once for the prosecutors. On their arrival, five days later, the trial began. The proceedings were probably in Latin, a language with which we must suppose St. Paul to be familiar, for he elected to defend himself. There were three counts in the indictment. The second, that of heresy (αἱρέσεως), was rather a matter of Jewish law. With this the prosecution linked two others, a charge of *majestas*, and an accusation of sacrilege, or profanation of their Temple. But the priests, strange to say, had overlooked the need of witnesses, two of whom at least by Roman law were necessary to prove the case. The rhetorician, Tertullus, did his best to secure condemnation by adroit flattery of the enfranchised slave, whom fortune had placed on the judgement-seat. But even Felix, who, in the words of Tacitus, 'exercised the power of a king with the temper of a slave,' dare not so degrade the law. By rights St. Paul should have been acquitted, but the procurator, whether in the hopes of a bribe or from a desire to conciliate the hierarchy, decided on a remand. He urged the absence of a material witness, the tribune Lysias.

For two years St. Paul lingered in prison. Felix was too busy dealing with the serious riots in Caesarea between Jew and Syrian to concern himself with St. Paul. But on the arrival of the new procurator, Festus, at the suit of the Jews a new trial was ordered. This second trial, though Festus himself was a better man than the degenerate Felix, was much more disorderly than the first. The forms of law were not observed, no witnesses were produced, and yet Festus, in his anxiety to please the Jews, offered to transfer the case to Jerusalem, and have it tried before the Sanhedrim as an ecclesiastical offence. St. Paul cut short this travesty of justice by an appeal to Caesar. After a short consultation the appeal was allowed. In spite of the inconvenience and expense, Festus could not do otherwise. Only if St. Paul had been taken in arms against the authorities could the procurator have quashed the appeal of a citizen. Doubtless, as Prof. Ramsay points out, 'the right of appeal was hedged in by fees and pledges.' This expense St. Paul must have met, possibly by the sale of his hereditary property. But Festus had as yet no specific charge to enter in the *litterae dimissoriae*, or *apostoli*, letters stating the case forwarded with the appellant. That he might fill up properly the charge-sheet (*elogium*), Festus laid the case before Agrippa and his sister Bernice. An informal hearing was arranged, and the prisoner introduced. In the middle of the Apostle's impassioned exhortation Festus interrupted the proceedings. Evidently St. Paul's books were turning his brain; but at any rate nothing criminal could be discovered for entry in the *elogium*. So with the well-known sneer of Agrippa at St. Paul's impulsiveness, or disregard of logic – the precise *nuance* is uncertain – the audience terminated.

The final issue of the appeal seems tolerably certain. After a delay of close upon three years, counting in the time occupied in the voyage to Rome, the case was heard. Of the causes of delay, as well as the parties to the prosecution, we know nothing. Even after the hearing had commenced there were many delays before the decision was given. But in his letter to the Philippians St. Paul was confident of the issue, and full of thankfulness for the way in which his trial had turned out already to the furtherance of the Gospel. The successive adjournments had enabled him to lay his case, not once nor twice, before the Supreme Court. He expects shortly to see both Philemon and Philippian brethren – not a word, be it noted, of any plans for a journey to Spain. The Apostle would be tried before Nero. The court would be a room of Nero's palace, not, however, the Golden House of later days. Associated with the emperor were twenty assessors, selected from the senators. Formerly the votes of the senators were taken by ballot. But Nero preferred to receive from each a written opinion, and on the next day to deliver his judgement in person. From the *Pastoral Epistles* we gather that Nero pronounced for acquittal. He could scarcely do otherwise on the *elogium* of Festus, though perhaps the length of the trial shows the powerful influences brought to bear against the Apostle. The matter was too palpably a Jewish squabble, another instance of the wild hatreds of this fanatical people, to be of much concern to the central authorities. Two years later this official indifference gave place to a contrary policy.

IV

The murders of St. Stephen and St. James, the persecution at Damascus and elsewhere, and the early imprisonments of St. Paul, were the results of Jewish hatred. The infant Church was now to experience the more dreaded enmity of the Empire. For the martyrdom of St. Peter and St. Paul the earliest evidence, thirty years at least after the event, is a letter – somewhat too rhetorical, alas! – from the Church of Rome to that of Corinth:

Let us come to the athletes who lived but lately, the noble examples of our own generation. ... Let us set before our eyes the good Apostles. There was Peter, who by reason of unrighteous jealousy endured not one nor two but many labours, and thus having borne his witness (μαρτυρήσας) went to his appointed place of glory. Paul also, by reason of jealousy and strife, pointed out the way to the prize of patient endurance. ... He won the noble renown which was the reward of his faith; having taught righteousness unto the whole world, and having reached the bounds of the West; and when he had borne his witness (μαρτυρήσας) before the rulers, so he departed from the world and went unto the holy place, having been found a noble pattern of patient endurance.

With the acquittal of St. Paul after his first captivity (A.D. 61) the Apostle vanishes, though as one immortal, from the pages of certain history. The rest, his journeys East and West, his sudden arrest at Troas or Nicopolis, his second entrance as a captive into Rome, the letters of this second captivity, the manner of his trial, the date of his death, are matters of dispute, the exact details of which in any case are lost. One thing, however, is clear from a comparison of Philippians with II Timothy. There had been in the interval a complete change in the policy towards Christianity of the Roman Government. This change was due, as we shall see, to the great fire of Rome (July, 64). As part of the persecution which then broke out, orders were given for the imprisonment of the Christian leaders. Poppaea, Tigellinus, and their Jewish friends were not likely to forget the prisoner of two years before. At the time St. Paul was away from Rome, but steps were instantly taken for his arrest. The Apostle was bought back to the city in the autumn or winter of 64. Very different was his entrance into Rome from that which had been his lot on the former memorable occasion. No kindly officer-courier now did his best to make things smooth for his captive. On the contrary, the police had not even allowed him time to find his overcoat or necessary documents. The just and humane Burrus was dead. No Christians came down the Appian Way to meet him; the fear of the awful terror still lay heavy upon them. Instead of his own hired lodging there would be a noisome dungeon. His friends had deserted him, some, as Demas, for fear of the persecution; others even had turned traitor and were willing to appear in court against him. He was hated by the mob, treated as a malefactor, and as such now put upon his trial. That he had a trial at all instead of the summary punishment of his brethren wit-nesses to the importance attached by the Government to a show of legal-ity in the persecution of the leader.

There seem to have been two counts in the indictment. By ancient rules each was tried separately. The first count probably, as Conybeare and Howson suggest, was complicity in the fire. But even the false witness of Alexander, the coppersmith, who had turned informer (*de-lator*) because of his recent excommunication by the Apostle, could not upset the alibi which St. Paul was able to establish. So on this charge he 'was delivered out of the mouth of the lion', a phrase which possibly may point to the trial taking place before Nero himself. In the interval between the two actions he wrote his immortal last words. He had 'fought the good fight', he had 'run his race'. He had no delusions, no hope save to depart and be with Christ. There remained the 'offering up', and then 'the crown of righteousness'. The second count was either *majestas* – almost anything could be brought under this head – or the new crime of being a Christian, the crime of 'the Name', in itself a mere variation, as we shall see later, of *majestas* or high treason. On this indictment there could be but one verdict.

Round St. Paul's last days legend has woven thick a web of fancy, unless indeed, as well may be, loving tradition has thus preserved for us the real facts. After his condemnation he would probably be confined in the dungeon of Roman citizens and captives of eminence, the famous Mamertine. In itself there is little, save perhaps the distance from Rome, to prevent us from accepting the story consecrated by long ages that St. Paul 'offered up' his life in the green and level spot, with low hills around it, about three miles from the city, known in those days as the Aquae Salviae, now as the Tre Fontane. As he left Rome, almost the last object upon which his eyes would rest would be the pyramid of Caius Cestius, in its origin a record of the luxury of the *jeunesse doreé*, which thus became 'a monument unconsciously erected by a pagan to the memory of a martyr' who suffered, like his Lord, 'without the gate'. As a Roman citizen Paul escaped the more cruel fate of his brethren, and died by the sword. According to tradition, a convert of distinction, Lucina by name, took away the body by night and buried it in her garden on the Ostian Way, where today stands in his name one of the most stately churches of Christendom.

Constantine, when he built the first basilica of St. Paul's, is said to have placed the body in a coffin of solid bronze. If so the coffin was stolen or destroyed, probably with its contents, at the time of the sack of the church by the Saracens in 846. All that can be seen today is a slab of marble, with the words somewhat rudely carved thereon—

PAVLO APOSTOLO MART.

But Western Christianity itself is really his monument.

The date and circumstances of the martyrdom of St. Peter are even more uncertain. According to an ancient story, the truth of which we see no reason to doubt, the Apostle saw his wife suffer first, one of the many victims of Nero's cruelty. 'Then was the blessed Peter glad because she had been called and was now going home. So he lifted up his voice and cried to her in an encouraging voice, addressing her by name, and saying, "O thou, remember the Lord". Such was the marriage of the blessed ones and their perfect love.'

Very beautiful is the story of St. Peter's own release, though, unfortunately, its historical value is not without doubt. When the persecution of Nero broke out, the Apostle, who had arrived in Rome, as we read it, towards the close of St. Paul's first captivity, was persuaded to flee. So in the dead of night Peter left the city, and hastened down the Appian Way. But when he came to a place where today there stands a chapel with the legend *Domine quo vadis*, then—

> Lo on the darkness brake a wandering ray;
> A vision flashed along the Appian Way.
> Divinely on the pagan night it shone –
> A mournful Face – a Figure hurrying on –
> Though haggard and dishevelled, frail and worn,
> A King, of David's lineage, crowned with thorn.
> 'Lord, whither farest?' Peter, wondering, cried,
> 'To Rome,' said Christ, 'to be re-crucified.'

'Whereupon Peter – we cite the Psuedo-Ambrose – 'perceived that Christ must be crucified a second time in his little servant. And he turned and went back and made answer to the Christians as they questioned him, and forthwith men laid hands upon him, and by his cross he glorified the Lord Jesus.'

Thus Peter, as our Lord had prophesied, was 'girt' by another, and 'carried' out to die along the Aurelian Way, to a place hard by the gardens of Nero on the Vatican hill. At his own request he was crucified head downwards, as unworthy to suffer like his Master. Where he died he was buried 'under a terebinth', close to the obelisk of Nero, where today the world's most splendid temple rises to his memory.

According to an old tradition, St. Peter had been accompanied to Rome by the Apostle John. He too was seized by the police and condemned to be plunged into a cauldron of boiling oil at a spot near the Latin Gate. By what Providence St. John escaped we know not, but in the Apocalypse as we interpret it, we have 'the cry of horror of a witness who has known the Beast, who has seen the bleeding bodies of his brother martyrs,' and who in his exile at Patmos tells us of the afflictions and consolations of the children of God. In his fierce song over the burning of Rome – in Patmos he dreamed not of the new magnificence with which Nero had rebuilt it – as well as in the hatred of the Empire which breathes through every page, we see clearly some of the reasons which explain the attitude of the Government to the Christians. Intensely Jewish as is the imagery and tone of the book as a whole, the Apocalypse, nevertheless, means the definite break of the Church and Judaism. In the new Jerusalem the Apostle saw 'no temple therein'; 'the ark of the covenant' is now in 'the temple of God that is in heaven'.

St. John's banishment to Patmos was itself a result of the great persecution of Nero. Hard labour for life in the mines and quarries of certain islands, especially Sardinia, formed one of the commonest punishments for Christians. The writer tells us that he was 'the brother and partaker with you in the tribulation,' of those who were suffering elsewhere for the sake of Christ, a statement which would appear to rule out voluntary retirement. At work in the quarries or engaged in other convict task – mines in the island there are none – the seer dreamed his dreams and saw his visions. He stood on the shore of the sea and beheld the Beast rise out of the waves, he saw the battle joined, he heard the clash of arms in heaven and hell, he rejoiced in victory won, and the descent of the City of God. In the long weary years of exile his faith in the future never grows faint; he brings in a new world to redress the balance of the old.

We know nothing of the events which secured St. John's release from this convict settlement. The fall of Domitian and the annulment of his acts may have led, as Clement of Alexandria tells us, to an amnesty for the Apostle, after a quarter of a century of suffering. More probably, in our judgement, he had been banished not so much by direct imperial as by magisterial sentence – perhaps by the magistrates of Ephesus – which in some way or other became reversed. There are grounds also for thinking that the Apostle returned from Patmos to Ephesus already his home before his exile, some years before the death of Domitian. But whatever the cause or date of his release, we believe that for the Apostle of love peace was

> The soft seal of long life's closing story.

He lived through the horrors of two great persecutions, and died quietly in extreme old age at Ephesus, possibly as late as the reign of Trajan—

> And now the man
> Lies as he lay once, breast to breast with God.

Chapter Two

CAESAR OR CHRIST

I

PERSECUTION in its origin must be ascribed to the Jews: it was really an attempt of the hierarchy to crush out the new sect. But within a few years persecution ceased to be Jewish, and became Imperial, thus realizing the determination of the Jews from Calvary onwards. In opposition to the infant Church there arose the might of Rome. The conflict was inevitable, the direct result of the genius of Christianity. A Christianity which had ceased to be aggressive would speedily have ceased to exist. Christ came not to send peace on earth but a sword; against the restless and resistless force of the new religion the gates of hell should not prevail. But polytheism could not be dethroned without a struggle; nor mankind regenerated without a baptism of blood. Persecution, in fact, is the other side of aggression, the inevitable outcome of a truly missionary spirit; the two are linked together as action and reaction. To the student of ancient history all this will appear intelligible, perhaps even axiomatic. 'The birth-throes of the new religion must needs be agonizing. The religion of the civilized world was passing through Medea's cauldron.' Out of the cauldron there would come a new world, but not without fire and blood. Persecution, in short, is no mere incident in the life of the Church which might possibly have been avoided. Not so do we read either history or Christianity. Persecution rather was the necessary antagonism of certain fundamental principles and policies in the Empire of Caesar and the Kingdom of Christ. But on this more anon. We shall do well first to clear up certain matters connected with the early martyrs which have given rise to much controversy. The date at which persecution began, the extent to which it prevailed, its exact legal character, are questions of moment to which we shall attempt a brief answer. We shall then be in a better position to explain the reasons for persecution and its true inwardness from the standpoint both of the Empire and the Church.

Scholars are now fairly agreed that by the time of Domitian it had become the settled policy of the Roman emperors, and of the wonderfully efficient police administration which they controlled, to treat Christianity as itself a crime. But in our judgement Domitian was not the originator of a new departure. The establishment of this policy in the first instance was due to Nero. On the evening of 19 July 64, there broke out in Rome a disastrous fire, the least effect of which was the burning down of no small part of the congested quarters of the city. The fire marks a crisis in the fortunes of the Church, the beginning of an era of persecution which lasted for over two centuries. In a well-known chapter of Tacitus – the meaning of which is by no means as clear as we should wish, though its genuineness seems beyond dispute – we read:

Neither human assistance in the shape of imperial gifts, nor attempts to appease the gods, could remove the sinister report that the fire was due to Nero's own order. And so, in the hope of dissipating this rumour, he falsely diverted the charge on to a set of people to whom the vulgar gave the name of Christians, and who were detested for the abominations which they perpetrated. The founder of this name, one Christus by name, had been executed by Pontius Pilate in the reign of Tiberius; and the dangerous superstition, though put down for the moment, again broke out, not only in Judea, the original home of the pest, but even in Rome, where everything horrible and shameful collects and is practised.

The charge of incendiarism broke down completely, both with the Roman judges and with the populace.

But

The lie

Had time on its own wings to fly,

and was made the occasion – not without some ground in the incautious utterances of enthusiastic Millenarians – of an accusation more dangerous by far, *odium generis humani*, 'hatred against civilized society', or, as we should phrase it today, the crime of anarchism. Not specific acts of incendiarism, but 'the question whether a man was a Christian, became the most essential part of the charge against him.'

The policy of thus treating the Christians as anarchists, begun by Nero, was continued – developed, perhaps, in some small details – by the Flavian emperors Titus and Domitian, and by the Antonines after them, as a cardinal principle of imperial government. In this they were aided by the revulsion of feeling which Christianity had aroused against itself among the masses of the people, and the rumours already current of its impure orgies. Long before the close of the century the prophecy of Christ had come true: the Christians were hated of all men 'because of the name' (Matt. 10: 22).

Leaps and bounds are as alien to history as in nature. We must not, therefore, imagine that Christianity suddenly became a persecuted religion in the year 64, though hitherto it had enjoyed a certain measure of protection, possibly even favour, from the Roman Government. True it is, as the Acts of the Apostles shows, and as Gibbon claims, that in the earlier days the Christians found that 'the tribunal of the pagan magistrates often proved the most assured refuge against the fury of the synagogue.' But the cause of this was not any official countenance of Christianity as such, but a careless indifference to what appeared the mere minutiae of Judaism. Judaism was a *religio licita*, and Christianity at first seems to have been confused with it and thus to have obtained a certain measure of protection as against the Gentiles from the authorities. But the hatred of the synagogues soon undeceived the Roman world, and persecution, instead of being, as hitherto, the work of the mob stirred up by Jewish gold, became the duty of the Empire. To this last, in fact, the bureaucracy was driven by the political charges which the Jews brought against the new sect, a weapon the value of which they had learned on Calvary.

We can date with some certainty this distinction in the official mind between Jew and Christian as first becoming clear in the summer of 64. The acquittal of St. Paul in 61 or 62 – an event we may fairly assume as probable – is proof that in that year Christianity, a distinct name for which was only slowly coming into use, could still claim that it was a *religio licita*, i.e. as St. James would have put it, still recognized as a branch of Judaism. But soon after, as Tacitus shows, Christians as such, as distinct from the Jews, came under the ban of the Empire. The Jews, working probably through Poppaea, the famous mistress and wife of Nero, whose superstitious nature led her to dally with Judaism, or through Aliturus, a favourite Jewish mime, took the opportunity of the great fire and the need of a scapegoat to save themselves and at the same time to wreak vengeance on the Christians. At any rate, both Nero and Rome now clearly distinguished between the *religio licita* of Judaism and the new sect, the majority of whose members possibly were already Gentiles.

The destruction of Jerusalem would remove the last elements of confusion. The breach between Judaism and Christianity was now complete, while the forced registration of all Jews, and the payment by them of two drachmas a head to the temple of Jupiter Capitolinus at Rome, would enable the officials to discover whether a Christian was or was not entitled to the protection of the *religio licita*. A more speedy method of identification was also available. The second generation of Christians, led by St. Paul, had distinguished circumcision. The Christians also, hitherto, distinguished by mere sub-titles of Judaism – The Way, Nazarenes, and the like – had now found, or rather had foisted upon them, a distinctive name of their own.

Many writers of repute have objected to the early date at which in our judgement the distinction became clear between Judaism and Christianity. Some extremists, constructing facts to suit their theories, have held that the two were confused until the time of Trajan; others, as a concession, have moved the date forward to Domitian. Such arguments do strange injustice both to the power of the Jews to make themselves understood, and to the vigilance of the officials of the most marvellously organized and centralized empire the world has ever seen. No reader, for instance, of the *Epistle of Barnabas*, could imagine that such violent hatred of the two sections would not make itself manifest to the lynx-eyed police; no historian who realized the vast numbers of the Jews and their world-wide power could suppose that the Jews allowed the hated sect to be classified with them. The English people, to say nothing of English governors, do not confuse Brahmins and Buddhists. Roman officials, we may be sure, would be quick to note the rise of a new sect. As Professor Lindsay points out:

When we remember the wise political dread of religious combinations which the emperors from Augustus downward showed; their discernment that religion was the most powerful political motive power in the East; the presence in every province of men trained to note the beginnings of all movements which might disturb the state: and when we glance at the objective picture of that old system of ruling provinces which modern India furnishes – none but an armchair critic would deny it. British officials in India know of all the small beginnings of religious movements in their districts long before the public know anything about them, if they ever acquire the knowledge.

If, then, we date the distinction between Jew and Christian as first becoming officially clear in or about the summer of the year 64, we can understand what really took place in the interesting case of Pomponia Graecina. This high-born Roman lady, the wife of Plautius, the conquerer of Britain, may claim with some certainty to have been the first Roman of whose sufferings for the sake of Christ we have any record. In the year 57 Pomponia was arraigned before the Senate on the charge of 'foreign superstition', and in accordance with usage, handed over by that court to the judgement of a family tribunal. She was acquitted, but for the remaining twenty-six years of her life never put off her seriousness of demeanour or her deep mourning. Critics of repute have claimed that this 'foreign superstition' was Christianity, and in the judgement of Lightfoot 'this surmise, probable in itself, has been converted almost into a certainty by an archaeological discovery of recent years.' For de Rossi has shown that in the so-called crypt of Lucina, a first-century fragment of the catacombs of Callistus, we have the name of a descendant or near kinsman of Pomponia Graecina. Evidently, then, there were Christians in her family within a generation of her trial. Furthermore, this crypt must have been built by a lady of rank and wealth, and as the name Lucina does not occur elsewhere in Roman history, De Rossi suggests that this is none other than the baptismal name of Pomponia Graecina, who, as Tacitus tells us, died in A.D. 83, or about the time of the erection of this crypt. If then, it may be objected, Pomponia was a Christian, how can we account for her acquittal? Wandinger's answer, adopted by Lightfoot, is ingenious and probable. The real matter referred to the judgement of the domestic tribunal was not her faith. This neither the Senate nor the family were careful to distinguish from Judaism, a recognized religion. She was really tried because of the rumours already abroad accusing the Christians of impure orgies, which shortly afterwards led to such an outburst of popular hatred.

Thus the fire of 64 did not create, but brought to a head the growing suspicion and dislike by both people and government of this new religion, and at the same time threw out into sharp relief its distinction from Judaism. Indecision on the part of the executive was now at an end; it was to the advantage of Nero, in his desperate need of popular favour, that it should be. In its place we have a policy of persecution. The persecution, though by no means widespread – Christianity itself, be it remembered, as yet only existed here and there – was not confined to Rome, but extended to various cities and districts of Asia Minor, rather, however, as a police-measure than because of any formal rescript. Within a generation of Calvary the sheep were in the midst of the wolves.

II

The imperial idea that Christianity was a danger to the State and civilization itself, an anarchist institution, was maintained with varying insistence, some modification in detail, and occasional intervals of toleration, from the days of Nero to the final victory of the Church under Constantine. To the changes and fortunes of this policy in the first three centuries, as also to the reasons which gave it plausibility and credence with both statesmen and people, we shall return later. Meanwhile the student should notice certain consequences of moment.

The charge of anarchism exposed the Christians to one peril in special. It put them outside the law and brought them under the arbitrary executive jurisdiction of the magistrates and police superintendents. These, as Mommsen has pointed out, were entrusted with large powers of immediate action (*coercitio*), on their own responsibility, against all persons whose conduct was likely to lead to political trouble. Just as in modern Russia the Nihilist or the innocent reformer can be arrested and sentenced, even banished for life to Sakhalien, on mere 'administrative order', without the pretence of trial, or the need that the bureaucrat quote any law at all, so with the early Christian. Their trial (*cognitio*) could be conducted in private, the results alone being made public. In the case of Christians torture and death were within the magistrates' competence, though curious to say, they were not allowed to inflict banishment (*deportatio*) until the time of Marcus Aurelius. And the penalty was fixed; 'in the case of base-born Christians (*humiliores*), the fighting with beasts in the arena, or the being burnt alive; in the case of Roman citizens (*honestiores*), the headsman's sword.'

The reader who has followed our argument will find an answer to the further question, Were persecutions the exception or the rule? In theory, Christianity was a hateful thing, a danger to society and the State, to be crushed out wherever found. In practice, vigilance varied considerably; there were spasms of enforcement of the law followed by reactions of indifference on the part of both Government and people. Persecution was also to a large extent a local matter; an outburst of popular hatred driving the magistrates to put into force enactments that would be distasteful to some if only because of the extra work that they involved, to others because of their consciousness of their futility. A modern illustration may make the matter clear. The Christian was looked upon very much as an Anarchist or Nihilist is looked upon by the police of Paris or St. Petersburg. He is kept under strict observation; the police can proceed against him any day without formality or delay. But because of that very fact the Anarchist is only arrested when popular feeling or his own doings demand. If he keeps quiet the police do not trouble him. So with the Christian. 'The current conceptions', writes Mommsen, 'of the so-called persecutions of the Christians labour under a defective apprehension of the rule of law and the practice of law subsisting in the Roman Empire. In reality the persecution of the Christians was a standing matter, as was that of robbers; only such regulations were put into practice at times more gently or even negligently, at other times more strictly, and were doubtless on occasion specially enforced from high quarters.' These times of 'enforcement from high quarters' formed the seasons of special stress and strain known to the historians of the Church as the 'General Persecutions.' To these likewise in due course we shall return. They have received an attention which by its very exaggeration has spread confusion. Of more importance is it that the student should realize that these 'general persecutions' are but, as it were, the coming to a head of a virulence against the Christians always more or less at work in the imperial system.

Another consequence of this main argument should be noted. Christianity, as we have seen, was put down as a police measure, by 'administrative order' rather than by formal laws, or stately trials. From the outlook of the later historian the result was disastrous. Police-court cases are not enrolled among the archives of the nation. A great trial, a Verres or a Warren Hastings, brings forth the orations, immortal not merely in themselves, but because of the light they throw upon current law or history. But no orator defended St. Paul or St. Perpetua; few records are preserved of the trials of insignificant Anarchists. The very laws under which they were prosecuted do not demean themselves to illustrations of their bearing and application at the hands of great jurists by instances gathered from the scum of society. Ulpian, Paulus, Modestinus – the Cokes and Lytteltons of the third century – leave the crime of Christianity as such alone; they saw no reason for singling it out from other moral enormities with which the police had ample powers of dealing. If only St. Paul or Ignatius had been a Verres or a Clodius – gigantic peculators, administrators whose tyranny set a province on fire, daring revolutionaries – all would have been clear, set forth with precision in the text-books of the schools. As it is, the historian is reduced to the scanty flotsam and jetsam thrown up from the sea of oblivion; a detail here, a fragment there from which we must reconstruct as best we may the great conflict between the Church and the Empire.

III

There was a second way in which the State might have tried to suppress the Christians other than by the method of treating them as outlaws and anarchists. The Empire, as distinct from the later Republic, was always jealous of all unregistered clubs and societies. We must own that the dread was not unwarranted, when we remember on the one hand the constant disaffection of the displaced oligarchy, and on the other the vast slave populations, the complex racial elements, and the smallness of the standing army by means of which peace was preserved. In the days of the Republic the only societies under the ban were those which met secretly or by night. But Julius Caesar, on political grounds, suppressed all sodalities except those of ancient origin, while Augustus placed all religious societies under the strictest control. Henceforth all new societies had to obtain permission either from the emperor or from the senate, according as they belonged to impartial or to senatorial provinces. Unregistered clubs could be suppressed by the police at any time;

though here again the power of suppression must not be confused with the deed itself. Probably clubs of all sorts would be allowed to meet, more or less openly recognized though without formal licence, the more so because the police knew that they could at any time put an end to their existence. By the *Lex Julia* (48 B.C.) members of unregistered clubs could be summarily punished by the police, if necessary with the extreme penalties of treason. But at the same time care was taken that such prohibition should not be a pecuniary benefit to the State. The common funds of a dissolved sodality were to be divided, not confiscated, a restriction which would not apply in the case of treason.

Of the jealousy of the Empire of the power of clubs and guilds we have several illustrations. In Nicomedeia, the future residence of Diocletian, one of the greatest cities of Asia Minor, a disastrous fire destroyed many dwellings, a club for old men, and a temple of Isis. The authorities applied for permission to form a fire brigade of 150 men. Pliny, the then governor of Bithynia-Pontus, who forwarded their request, promised that he would take care 'that no workman should be received into the brigade, and that it would not be used for other purposes.' But Trajan dreaded clubs more than fires, and so refused. Nor would he allow the citizens of Amisus to continue their subscription suppers. Trades unions too were considered illegal; not until the time of Septimius Severus did they obtain any legal status, though here again the student should beware of confusing legal recognition with absence of existence. Their recognition was the result of accomplished facts which it were idle for wise statesmen any longer to deny.

For these rigid restrictions overshot themselves and proved impossible. Laws and ordinances were paralysed by greater though impalpable forces; the universal craving for mutual sympathy and succour; the immense development of a free proletariat with collective interests of its own; above all the intense desire of the people to obtain relief from the deadly dullness of their lives. For 'the Empire which had striven to prevent combination, really furnished the greatest incentive to combine. In the face of that world-wide and all-powerful system, the individual subject felt, ever more and more, his loneliness and helplessness.' So, slowly but surely, the people asserted for themselves the right to organize societies, though under restrictions jealously guarded, in theory at least, down to the time of Justinian.

Thus the age of the infant Church became an age of clubs and guilds, of efforts in various ways to attain the new ideas of unity and brotherhood. There were clubs and sodalities of all sorts – colleges of old men and of young men, of wandering traders and military veterans, and of artisans in almost every conceivable branch of industry or specialized skill, from the mule-drivers of the Alps to the men whose business it was to strew the fine sand in the arena. The Great Mother, Isis, Serapis, and other gods, all alike had their colleges; religion, in fact, played no small part in this vast club life. We have also one sodality at least that was virtually a White Cross Guild, though this must be balanced by the sodalities of the 'late sleepers' and 'late drinkers' at Pompeji. As Mommsen showed in one of his earliest works, it was not difficult for any society desirous of making contributions for any purpose, to enroll itself under forms allowed by law, though freedom was somewhat narrowed by the fact that meetings were only allowed once a month, and that no permanent head, or 'master of sacred rites', could be appointed. Owing to these last restrictions, perhaps, or from unwillingness to lower their religion to the level of a sodality or mutual benefit club, or because they were aware that there were many religious clubs which had received no licence and yet existed, the early Christians either refused or neglected the opportunity and freedom of such registration, while their ἀγάπαι, or love-feasts – which would appear to have existed longer than is sometimes supposed – would make them an illegal sodality the crushing of which would need no further formalities. As a matter of fact, the States preferred, as a rule, to proceed against the Christians, not as members of an illegal guild, but as political agitators or anarchists of the most dangerous form. We have proof of this in the fact that at the commencement of the third century, when the Christians here and there took steps, apparently, to enroll themselves as burial clubs, the persecutions did not thereby cease. The Christians were punished, not as members of an illicit sodality, but 'for the Name'.

The student should beware, however, lest he overlook the momentous issues involved in the refusal of the State to allow any society or club to exist which had not first obtained official recognition, and the equally momentous refusal of the Church to obtain such recognition. The question is not one of legal technicalities or procedure, or the 'sheer obstinacy', as Marcus Aurelius would have phrased it, of Christian fanatics, but points rather to one of those root antagonisms of principle the influence of which, in different forms, may be felt in the twentieth as much as in the second century. By Roman theory the State was the one society which must engross every interest of its subjects, religious, social, political, humanitarian, with the one possible exception of the family. There was no room in Roman law for the existence, much less the development on its own lines of organic growth, of any corporation or society which did not recognize itself from the first as a mere department or auxiliary of the State. The State was all and in all, the one organism with a life of its own. Such a theory the Church, as the living kingdom of Jesus, could not possibly accept either in the first century or the twentieth. Here, in fact, we strike a root antagonism of political ideals between the Church and the Empire, the details and consequences of which will need further examination. Suffice to say that this was not the least of the factors which led from the first to an outbreak of persecution.

IV

To the modern reader the crime of anarchism thus alleged against Christianity seems so preposterous, that he finds it hard to believe that such a charge could ever have been seriously entertained. Nothing, in fact, is more difficult in the study of history than to put oneself back into the thoughts and feelings of past centuries, and to view events from a standpoint the very foundations of which have utterly perished. The student who succeeds in doing this in his investigation of the relations in early days of the Church and the Empire will discover that the notion was not so utterly absurd after all as at first sight it appears. To both people and bureaucrat the Christians would seem, if not exactly Anarchists, yet something scarcely distinguishable. History, the judge from whose verdicts there is no appeal, has shown that the statesmen and magistrates of the Empire were wrong, as history has exposed similar follies in every century. Nevertheless, the astute rulers of the Empire did not adopt their views without reasons which on the surface appeared sufficient. What these were we shall explain in a later chapter.

The difficulty of the reader in understanding this charge is increased when he remembers the known tolerance of the Roman Empire for all sorts of religions. For the city had slowly adopted as her own, by senatorial decree or popular verdict, a vast pantheon of other gods; not merely Italian deities, Juno and Diana, or the gods of Greece, Apollo, Athene, but Oriental deities, such as the Great Mother, and the worship of Mithra. The belief in the old Roman deities that had contented the rude farmers of Latium had slowly melted away under the solvent of Greek philosophy and world-wide conquest; their places had been taken by alien mythologies of larger human interest and more alluring legend. Not only had strangers introduced into the great city the various superstitions of their native countries, but Rome herself had bestowed 'the freedom of the city on all the gods of mankind'. Orontes had flowed into the Tiber; but the Tiber had seemed no less anxious to receive her. In the case of some of these adopted or imported gods the rites were not always remarkable for their moral power. And yet the worship of Isis, though never formally adopted by the State, was allowed, in spite of attendant orgies; that of Jesus was forbidden. The licentious rites of Adonis were the glory and disgrace of Antioch; the brotherhood in Christ Jesus was under the ban of the Empire. The cult of Aesculapius (a foreign deity introduced from Epidaurus, on the advice of the Sibylline books, as far back as 290 B.C. – 'God the Saviour', 'the friend of man' ($\phi\iota\lambda\alpha\nu\theta\rho\omega\pi\acute{o}\tau\alpha\tau\sigma$) – was especially popular, as his numerous inscriptions and statues testify. The worship of 'the great Physician' 'who went about doing good' was suppressed. How came these things to be, the reader asks? By what perversion of logic or fact did it come to pass that an Empire so tolerant in its general practice could be so hostile to the Church? Is it that the toleration of the Empire was less complete than is supposed, or has the measure of the persecutions of the Christians been exaggerated by ecclesiastical zealots?

The answer to these questions cannot be given in a simple yes or no. We must distinguish between things that differ; for instance, the liberty of thought and the liberty of worship. Liberty of thought, so far as the Government was concerned, was complete, far more so than in the latter days of Giordano Bruno, Servetus, or Galileo. The *theologicum odium* did not exist, at any rate in Rome, if only because men were not sufficiently interested in their gods to make them a battle-ground. But liberty of worship was a different matter, depending chiefly on political and local considerations. The rites allowed, or even favoured, in Phrygia or Gaul could not be equally tolerated elsewhere. In this matter the Romans, like most great imperial administrators, were opportunists. In Jerusalem they protected the worship of Jehovah; the Roman who passed within the portals of the temple was put to death. In Ephesus they were equally ready in the interests of Artemis to crucify the Jew. Political expediency rather than abstract theory lay at the root of their system of toleration, or rather protection, of local deities. For the same administrative reasons Rome, the centre of the world, the great meeting-place of all nations and ages, the fountain of honour, welcomed within her borders, under certain restrictions, the deities of all her subject nations. Whatever he might think in his heart, in his public utterance the Roman was not guilty of the scornful folly of a Sennacherib. The wrath of a Cambyses pouring itself out in the destruction of the embalmed bulls and shrines of Egypt did not seem to him the best model for attaching Egypt to the imperial city; nor would the nations love Rome the more if the stranger visiting the capital should find himself cut off from the rites with which he was familiar. But it was all a matter of political expediency and administrative fitness; toleration as a philosophical theory never entered Roman thoughts.

For this very reason we must not forget that the toleration of Rome was always less complete than is sometimes claimed. Especially was this the case in the early Republic. From Livy's account of the Bacchanalian scandal in 186 B.C., we see the sternness with which the executive put down all religious associations that tended to become a danger to the State or to morals, while even in later and looser days no new worship was allowed to be introduced 'except by decree of the Emperor ratified by the Senate'. But this last was the very thing that for Christianity, as for Judaism before it, was an impossibility. Christ could not be one among many; His claims rested upon higher grounds than senatorial allowance. Furthermore, even when a religion was tolerated, Roman citizens, in theory at any rate, might not participate in it, whatever was allowed to the alien. For the Roman citizen whatever went beyond the prescription of ancestral worship fell under the definition of 'superstition'. We have an illustration of this in the case of the worship of the Great Mother. Though formally adopted by the Senate in 204 B.C., not for a century were Roman citizens permitted to join its priesthood. In Egypt Augustus revered the majesty of Isis; nevertheless Augustus prohibited the worship within a mile of the sacred *pomerium*.

Thus when political considerations demanded the Romans crushed out remorselessly religion or rites which seemed to them to stand in their way. We have an illustration of this in the case of Druidism. The political power of this religion, the resistance to Roman rule that found a head in the priests, was felt to be too great. Hence, though Augustus had tolerated the faith, steps were taken by Tiberius and Claudius for suppressing the great annual meeting of the Druids at the centre of their cult, the hill of Chartres. As part of the same plan, it was determined to occupy the Druid strongholds in Britain. An excuse was found, if any were needed, in the traffic in charms carried on by the priests, the annual human sacrifices in great wickerwork pens, and the healing of the sick by the flesh of the slain. The result was seen in the rapid Romanization of Celtic Gaul.

Nor must we forget that the toleration of Rome, such as it was, was nearer akin to contempt and indifference. Now, the toleration which springs from contempt is often intensely intolerant of one thing, namely, of enthusiasm, using the word in a sense better understood and disliked in the eighteenth century than to-day. 'What a fool you are,' said Maximus the judge to the veteran Julius, 'to make more of a crucified man than of living emperors;' nor would his contempt be lessened by the answer of Julius: 'He died for our sins that He might give us eternal life'. 'Sacrifice and live, then,' retorted Maximus. 'If I choose life,' replied the veteran, 'I choose death; if I die, I live for ever.' At this Maximus, who hitherto had been most anxious to save so old a soldier, lost his temper.

He would feel that in sentencing the man to death he was ridding the earth of a madman. We see this contempt of enthusiasm breaking out time after time; in the sneers of Pilate and Agrippa, in the satires of Lucian, and in the acts and sayings of magistrates and governors for nearly three centuries.

The idea of toleration may therefore be dismissed. The whole conception was yet unborn; many centuries would elapse before it should arise. Nor was toleration, when it came, due to the influence or example of the Church. The so-called toleration of Rome was founded in reality upon political expediency. But a toleration founded on political expediency must always at some point or other, if only it is logical, become intolerant. From the utilitarian standpoint the policy of a Pobiedonostseff has much to plead on its own behalf. Expediency demands, for the sake of unity, that the Stundists or Old Believers be crushed out, though at the same time the heathenism of the tribes that dwell on the barren tundras of Siberia may receive recognition, at any rate for the nonce. So in Rome. A wise recognition of local usages was one thing, provided always that the interests of the State were duly conserved; a toleration founded upon the claims of conscience and the rights of the individual soul was a matter too absurd even for philosophers to discuss.

The reader will not fail to notice one result. Toleration was a local matter, if only for the simple reason that polytheism was essentially a local matter. Each god had his rights, within certain areas; but each god must be careful to respect the rights of his neighbour. To ignore this rule would lead to chaos, or rather the end of the whole system. A universal faith, provided it makes any real demands on its devotees, must come into conflict with polytheism. The claims of the local and of the universal cannot be conciliated. We see this in later days in the case of Muhammad. The same thing was illustrated even more abundantly in the rise of the Church. The Christians were not persecuted because of their creed, but because of their universal claims. For monotheism, viewed merely as a philosophy, the Romans had some sympathy. But a monotheism which refused to allow place for others must be brushed aside as a political nuisance or 'atheistic' monster. This universality of claim, this aggressiveness of temper, this consciousness from the first of world-wide dominion – in a word, all that in later days was summed up in the title of Catholic – was the inevitable cause of Roman persecution. Neither the Church nor the Empire could act otherwise save by running contrary to their true genius. The failure to understand this essential opposition lies at the root of the constant complaints of Christian apologists as to the different treatment measured out to them and 'to the men who worship trees and rivers and mice and cats and crocodiles'.

V

We have referred already to the toleration by the State of the worship of Isis and Mithra. On deeper examination the contradiction between this toleration and the persecution of Christianity disappears; their history, in fact, is seen to run on somewhat parallel lines, and to afford illustration rather than contradiction. The worship of Isis won its way to recognition in the face of fierce opposition; its story is the story of a popular religious movement of Eastern origin in perpetual conflict with Roman conservatism. Time after time the temples of Isis were destroyed only to be re-erected on a larger scale by popular enthusiasm and the growing cosmopolitanism. Slaves and freed men especially those from Egypt, were the apostles of the new faith long before it became fashionable in higher circles. Not until the latter years of the first century of our era did Isis succeed in obtaining the sanction and worship of the bureaucracy itself.

Even more valuable as an illustration both in its arguments and differences is the case of Mithraism, the greatest rival which Christianity ever had to face. In some respects Christianity and Mithraism were curiously alike. Both religions were of Eastern origin. Both religions had entered Europe much about the same time, with the advantage of a few years in favour of Mithraism. Both religions possessed a strongly developed ecclesiastical organization, and emphasized the value of mysteries or sacraments, these last in some of their details strangely similar. Both religions were treated with scorn and indifference by the historians, poets, and philosophers of the Empire.

The worship of Mithra was one of the oldest cults of the Aryan race, in its origin identical with the worship of the sun. Adopted by the Persians, Mithra found a place in the Zoroastrian system, occupying a middle place between Ormuzd, who dwelt in eternal light, and Ahriman, whose sphere was darkness. In time Mithra became regarded as the viceroy on earth of the supreme deity, whose serene bliss no mortal cares could disturb. As his viceroy, Mithra was 'the Saviour', the head of the celestial armies in their ceaseless combat with the Spirit of Darkness. His 'invincible' might – the adjective is almost an inseparable – causes Ahriman himself in the depth of hell to tremble with fear. It is as the 'Saviour', the conqueror of Ahriman, that we see Mithra represented in a thousand inscriptions from Scotland to Egypt, with his sword buried in the neck of a bull.

In Europe the growth of Mithraism, almost contemporary with that of Christianity, seems to have run pretty much the same course, reaching its climax in the third century. We find its first home in the seaports; its earliest devotees were aliens and Syrian slaves. Thus in Ostia, the port of Rome, there were at least four shrines of Mithra. In Rome, the caravansary of the Empire, Mithraism reared a temple in the sacred Capitol itself. But a more interesting evidence of its strength lies in the fact revealed by de Rossi, that the oldest Church of St. Clement, the crypt of the present building (originally in all probability an early Christian chapel of the aristocratic family which in the year 95 gave Domitilla and her husband, the consul, to the Church), seems at a later date to have lapsed into a Mithraic shrine. The well-known bas-reliefs of Mithra in his birth from the rock may still be seen cut in its walls.

Mithra possessed one potent missionary agency which Christianity lacked. The stronghold of the former creed lay in the army. Not without good reason was the name of *milites* given to a certain grade of its initiates. In the second and third centuries the rank and file of the regular legions of the Roman army were for the most part stationary (*stationarii*). They were not liable for service, save in their own native province. But the centurions were always on the move, as were also the foreign auxiliaries of Eastern origin, with whom the cult of Mithraism originated. As they were quartered here and there throughout the world, centurions and auxiliaries erected their temples and devotional tablets, and spread abroad the gospel of their 'invincible Saviour'. From the army the worship was carried to the Court and the educated classes. Throughout the third century Mithra had his chaplains in the palace of Caesar. Commodus was enrolled among his adepts; Diocletian and Galerius, the great enemies of Christianity, dedicated to Mithra many temples; while Aurelian and Julian the Apostate sought to make Mithraism, or a variation thereof, the official cult. The Court, in fact, found in its doctrines that support for the autocracy which Christianity, as we shall see, refused to give. But the worship was by no means confined to the army and Court. Mithra possessed a second line of missionaries in the slaves of Eastern origin, the commonest article on the slave markets of Europe, who carried its cult to the obscurest corners of the Empire. An inscription at Nersae, in the heart of the Apennines, recounts how a slave, who had worked his way up into the position of treasurer of the town, in the year 172 restored the temple of Mithra, one only of many evidences of the activity of these servile missionaries.

With this introduction we may now face the question: How was it that of the two religions the one was persecuted, the other tolerated? The answer is most pertinent to our theme. Mithraism escaped persecution by taking refuge from its earliest days under the shelter of a *religio licita*, the worship of the Great Mother, with which it had many points of contact. Christianity, on the other hand, was not only driven out from the shelter of Judaism, but the Jews became its deadliest foes. Mithraism, moreover, early took advantage of the privileges afforded by enrolling its congregations as members of funerary societies. But the third reason is the most important. The worships of Isis and Mithra were by no means local cults; they too aspired to world-wide homage. But their strength lay in their power of absorbing and assimilating the best elements in surrounding paganism. They were willing not only to live and let live, but to take up and make part of themselves whatever feature of local religion, Christianity included, seemed especially popular or serviceable. 'Et ipse pileatus, Christianus est' – 'That man with the Mithraic cap is a Christian,' said a priest of Mithra to St. Augustine, who shrank back in horror from this attempt to identify his faith with this 'devil's imitation'. The Mithraic priest knew what he was about. The strength of Mithra and Isis lay in the current syncretism, that tendency to find unity and identity amid the multitudinous details of polytheism, the most familiar example of which is the identification of the gods of Greece and Rome. But for Christianity this compromise with other faiths, this syncretism, practical or philosophic, was an impossibility, at any rate in its earlier and purer days. With sublime audacity the followers of Jesus proclaimed that Christ must be all and in all. Once more we come back by a different route to the same cause of persecution, the essential absoluteness of the Christian faith. Christianity emblazoned on its banners its loathing and disdain for the cults around. 'We know that no idol is anything in the world, and that there is no God but one.' And the Christians demonstrated their convictions by the logic of the rack and the stake. We today, who suffer from the curse of a compromise with the world which gnaws at the heart of the Church, could not wish it otherwise. An accommodated Christianity would never have conquered the world.

Nor must we overlook in this connexion a factor of great importance. The advent of Christianity coincided with a great spiritual movement in the heathen world, which showed itself, not merely in the rapid spread of the newer cults, the worship of Isis, Mithra, and the like, but in the revival of belief in the older faiths and forms; above all in the growth throughout Europe of a social conscience. We see this awakened spiritual life in the guilds and charities, the constant efforts to extend and endow education, to found orphanages and hospitals, to emancipate women, and to rescue the slave from the unlimited power of his lord, which form the nobler features of the legislation of the Antonines, sad persecutors though they were of the Church of Jesus. That this upward movement of thought and creed, of which Mithraism was the best expression, undoubtedly helped the ultimate triumph of Christianity seems to us a certainty; nay, who shall say that this upward movement was not the work of the Spirit fulfilling Himself in diverse ways? But its first effects were far otherwise. During the later years of the Republic the old religion had almost fallen into decay; scores of temples were abandoned, priesthoods unfilled, the very names of the gods, as Varro tells us, recalled with difficulty. For political reasons the Empire set itself, as we shall see later, to the revival of the neglected religion, the rehabilitation of the ancient sacred colleges of Rome. The antique ritual of the Arval brotherhood was made a potent support of the imperial power; the worship of Jupiter received at the hands of philosophers a new meaning and strength; while the secular games in honour of Dis and Proserpine were revived and celebrated with a wealth and magnificence which baffles description, Horace himself writing a notable hymn for the occasion. With all this revival of old religions and belief Christianity, in the nature of things, was bound to come into conflict. By a correct instinct paganisms of all sorts discerned in the infant Church their only rival. So, while the new Hercules was yet in the cradle, they sent their snakes to kill him. But Hercules lived to cleanse out the Augean stalls.

VI

We may approach this argument with the same result, from another direction. Religion to the Roman was chiefly a matter of patriotism. The ecstatic emotions that we are accustomed to associate with the idea, the spiritual elevation, the recognition in divers forms of the unseen world and its claims, for him had little, if any, existence. But of one thing he was certain: no one could be a patriot who did not show due honour to the national gods. To refuse to do this was to bring upon oneself the charge of 'atheism' or 'sacrilege'. Belief or unbelief, correspondence between act and conviction, was beside the mark; as regards this the gods could defend themselves. As the schoolman would have phrased it, the sole concern of the State was with the *opus operatum*, the adequate discharge of the formal duty. The rest scarcely counted: 'the various modes of worship which prevailed in the Roman world were all considered by the people as equally true; by the philosopher as equally false; and by the magistrates as equally useful.'

Whatever the other truth that may underlie this sneer of Gibbon, the last clause is correct. To the Roman magistrate religious recusancy was practically tantamount to political disaffection. 'The introduction of strange divinities,' said Maecenas to Augustus, 'visit at once with hatred and chastisement ... for from this cause conspiracies and combinations and secret conspiracies are formed which are by no means expedient for a monarchy.' The whole speech is probably imaginary; none the less, Augustus acted in the spirit of the advice, while his successors, with few exceptions, identified themselves with his policy. They recognized that a wise conservatism in matters religious tended to the stability of the body political. One great exception they made. They left the local gods their rights, but established alongside of their worship a new imperial religion to serve, in the words of Mommsen, as 'the spiritual symbol of the political union.' The claims of this new religion, the nature of which we shall explain later, they insisted should be acknowledged universally. The only exception they made was the Jews.

Now it was precisely this religious recusancy, between which and rebellion the Roman judge could see but little difference, that Christianity demanded from all. The Church spurned the claims both of the local gods and of the new religion, the foundation and symbol of the Empire. 'The foundation was sapped, the symbol rejected by the Christians, and by the Christians first and alone.' To the Roman governor it was the Christian, not himself, that was intolerant. Whether or not Christians worshipped a crucified ass, as popular rumour had it, was a matter of profound indifference to the governor, provided only the Christian would take his part as a citizen in discharging the dues of the national gods, or at least allow others to do so without his interference. Said the Prefect of Alexandria to Dionysius, its bishop, whom he was anxious to save from the lions, 'What prevents you from worshipping this one god of yours, together with those that are the natural [sic] gods?' 'We worship,' was the reply, 'no other.' It was this absoluteness of the Christian faith, this intolerance of others, as the Romans considered it, that led to its being charged with anarchism because of its necessarily dissolvent effects on both the current religions and the political unity. For this anarchism on its religious side the Romans had a special name. They called it sacrilege, or atheism.

From his own standpoint the Roman was right. The Christians were 'atheists' (ἄθεοι, 'men without gods'), who proclaimed loudly that the gods – radiant Apollo, 'the Saviour' Aesculapius, even Jupiter Capitolinus himself – were but malignant 'demons' ensconced behind wood and stone; the imps of Satan, who had thus introduced the worship of themselves in order, to quote Tertullian, 'that they might obtain their favourite food of flesh fumes and blood.' Other Christian writers and preachers were not quite so 'atheistic'. The gods, they said, were ancient kings who in times prehistoric obtained apotheosis. But this more charitable view was held by few. The science of comparative religion was yet unborn. The majority held that it was a devil-ridden world, whose temples and shrines, however majestic, were among the works of darkness which Christ came to destroy, and which His followers also must seek to overturn, if necessary, by physical force and outrage. With these hordes of hell there could be no compromise: 'though there be that are called gods, yet to us there is one God the Father, of whom are all things, and we unto Him; and one Lord Jesus Christ, through whom are all things and we through Him.' This was the foundation of the faith, the first article of their creed. We can scarcely wonder that the Romans called such uncompromising monotheists by the hard name of 'atheists'. The Christians, they said, reduce our deities to devils. 'They despise the temples as dead houses, they scorn the gods, they mock sacred things.' To this charge there was no possible answer, inasmuch as it was true; the glory and danger of the Christian faith.

There was another way, of lesser importance, in which the Christians seemed to be 'atheists'. Strange as it seems to us today, Christian monotheism did not altogether appeal to some thinkers. The pagan Caecilius complains that the Christians made the heavens a wilderness and solitude with their 'one god, lonely and forsaken' – 'deus unicus, solitarius, destitutus' – the unutterable isolation and aloofness of whose position in heaven was fitly represented by his service on earth, 'who has neither temples, altars, victims, nor ceremonies.' To the Greek mind this 'lonely heaven' seemed an 'atheistic' impossibility. Polytheism, it is true, in the sense of a number of gods of equal power, was a discarded theory. As Plutarch and Maximus of Tyre are ever insisting, there must be one god supreme above all others. But this did not prevent belief in the existence of lesser deities, 'mediatised gods', as Dr. Bigg calls them, borrowing a figure from the relation in the German Empire of the lesser kings to the Emperor. All this hierarchy, with the underlying conception of the 'monarchy' of one god, Christianity swept away. 'The heathen', writes Tertullian, 'hurl in our teeth that we preach two gods or three gods . . . We, say they, maintain the monarchy.' Some maintained the 'monarchy' by means of a theory of 'daemons', partly human and part divine, which degenerated with the vulgar into the wildest pantheism. Others, for instance Porphyry, reasoned more boldly still against the Christian conception:

Let us proceed to inquire explicitly about the monarchy of the one God, and the joint-rule of those deities who are worshipped. . . . A monarch is not one who is alone, but one who rules alone over subjects of kindred nature with himself; as the Emperor Hadrian for instance, who was a monarch, not because he stood alone, or because he ruled cattle or sheep, but because he was king over human beings of like nature with his own.

To men of this way of thinking Christianity was bound to seem a choice between tritheism and 'atheism'. For the most part they chose the latter.

VII

The religious system of the Empire was thus built upon a foundation of liberty for local cults, a very different thing from toleration of a Catholic Church. Within certain limits the stranger might carry his worship and ritual with him when he moved to another portion of the Roman world. But to obtain this freedom he must be willing to live and let live, and to abstain, if needful, from proselytizing zeal. All was local, and yet at the same time all was universal. For Augustus, the better to work out those ideas of universal citizenship, equality, and government for which the Empire stood, had found it necessary to institute, or rather develop, throughout the Empire, a common religion to give a unity to provinces otherwise diverse in creed, language, and custom. This was the beginning of a universal church with a priesthood, sacrifices, and temples of its own, in conception and aim very similar and yet very different from the Catholic Church with which it was destined to come into conflict. But, such as it was, the worship of Rome and Augustus undoubtedly supplied something, which the local polytheisms had failed to give, a common religious link holding together the innumerable races and creeds of a dominion that stretched from the Irish Sea to the Euphrates. In connexion with this new worship there grew up a system of festivals and games, the conduct and cost of which fell to the lot of the president of the provincial diet (in Asia called Asiarch, in Galatia the Galatarch, and so on), though in many places endowments for the purpose were soon provided by the zeal of individual citizens or towns.

The worship of Rome and Augustus speedily became a fixed part of the imperial economy, in the development of which the servile cities of Asia vied with each other. Domitian took the matter so seriously, that he ordered all official proclamations to begin with formulae recognizing his deity. In Asia the temple of Rome and Augustus was first erected in 29 B.C. at Pergamum, the official capital of the province, 'where the throne of Satan is'. The writer of the Apocalypse has handed down to us the name of one brave Christian, Antipas, who suffered death there rather than join in the worship of 'the Beast'. With the decay of Pergamum the great city of Smyrna, the home of Polycarp, became the head centre of the new cult. Within a few years all the chief places of judicial circuit in Asia had their temples to Caesar, and their festivals in his honour. Their proudest boast was the confirmation upon them by the diet of the province of the title of 'Keeper of the Imperial Temple'. On the death of

Tiberius eleven cities of Asia struggled for the honour of erecting a temple to his memory. From Asia the worship spread to every province of the Empire. There was a temple to Claudius erected at Colchester during his lifetime, the costly ritual of which was one of the causes of Boudicca's revolt. In the West the new religion was little more than a matter of magnificent patriotic ceremonial. But in the East there existed 'a tendency to give reality to this imperial cult by identifying the divine Emperor with the local god, whatever form the latter had.'

This apotheosis was not limited to the reigning Caesar, but was extended to his family and favourites. Coins still exist testifying to the deification of no less than forty-eight members of the imperial families, including the shameless Faustina. The worst case of all was the consecration by Hadrian of his vicious favourite – the word is a euphemism – Antinoüs, after his mysterious death in the Nile. 'All men,' says Justin, 'were eager through fear to reverence him as a god, though they knew who he was and whence he had sprung.' 'His statues rose in every market-place; his soul was supposed to have found a home in a new star in the region of the Milky Way; temples were built in his honour, and the strange cult was maintained for at least one hundred years after any motive could be found for adulation.' The obelisk now on Monte Pincio at Rome was dedicated to his memory; in Egypt a town called Besantinopolis made him their special deity, while at Lanuvium, the burial-club of the place – whose rules by rare fortune we still possess – combined their other functions with the worship of Antinoüs and Diana.

The Christians alone stood out against this mark of a theocratic despotism. Whatever the political value of the new cult in the consolidation of the Empire, they would never bow the knee to the emperors, around whose heads, from the days of Nero onwards, were gilded darting rays in token of their divine solar ancestry. No patriotic words as to the Genius of the Empire, no sophisms of the elder Pliny that 'for a mortal to help mortals is the essence of deity,' no philosopic subtleties about the divine life of the State and its connexion with an unseen order, could deceive the Christian into forgetting the degradation for God and man alike of this system of apotheosis. He saw clearly the insult to God; the putting the Genius of the Empire in the place of Divine Providence, the attributing to man prerogatives which belong solely to the Almighty. He realized the degradation of man resulting from thus fixing the worship of men upon one of themselves, however exalted. He knew that in all ages a man's views of his god are the measures of his ideals for himself and his neighbour. He was aware of all that could be said in its favour; that it was a symbol of unity, the 'keystone of the imperial policy', an incarnation of the race's solidarity, the recognition of a divine foundation for order and empire, and the like. Such specious arguments did not move him. For the Christian there was but one Lord and Master, to whom he owned supreme allegiance; this he was prepared to prove by the renunciation of all things, even life itself. For the Christian the unity of the race was symbolized not by a Tiberius or a Marcus Aurelius, but by the incarnation of Jesus Christ; in the Man Christ Jesus alone was the hope of humanity. This apotheosis of Jesus, to look at the matter for the moment from the standpoint of the heathen philosopher, he claimed to be on a different footing from the apotheosis of Claudius or Vespasian. Leaving on one side all question of character, the one was the apotheosis of a supreme renunciation, the other the idolatry of success. And there is nothing so fatal in the long run to all higher instincts and aspirations as the idolatry of success, whether in the form of a second-century emperor or a twentieth-century millionaire.

This imperial cult, because of its universal character and obligations, thus furnished an easy touchstone whereby the Christians could be distinguished; a matter beyond the power of merely local polytheisms. Moreover, it proved a useful means of summary conviction. The alternative, 'Caesar is Lord' and 'Christ is Lord', was in itself a judicial process, only needing an altar and its usual emblems to be complete. The Christian who refused this sacrifice fell automatically under the charge of *majestas*, i.e. of mortal insult or treason to the Emperor, who represented in his own person the majesty, wisdom, and beneficent power of Rome. Nor was the peril slight. The Asiarch, Galatarch, and other presidents of the diets, were armed with ample powers for calling in the aid of the secular arm against all who refused to take part in this popular cult.

We can thus see how it came to pass that the annual festivals instituted in every province of the Empire on the Emperor's name-day were generally the occasions for the breaking out against the Christians of the smouldering fires of hatred and persecution. On these days the magistrates, even if otherwise averse to cruelty, were not anxious, for political reasons, to restrain the people from their exhibitions of loyalty. The festival of Caesar supplied all that was needed; vast crowds gathered together from every city of the province; the presence of the official diets and of judges with power of summary conviction, spurred on too by the sense of personal affront to themselves as the high-priests of the new ritual; beasts of prey already procured for the games – a most important point this, lions and tigers were not always in stock – a frenzied jingoism on the part of the mob, and an endeavour on the part of the Jews to divert attention from themselves and their prejudices to the hated Christian. Of this connexion we have an illustration in the martyrdom of Polycarp, who was burned at Smyrna on Caesar's festival, 23 February

155, 'in the consulship of Statius Quadratus, but in the reign of the Eternal King.'

'In the reign of the Eternal King' – the phrase occurs again and again in the records of the martyrs. The instinct which led one Christian Church when writing to another to describe itself as 'The Church which has its transitory home' at Lyons or elsewhere, reveals itself again in this scorn of the temporal *sub specie aeternitatis*. Martyrdom might be the inevitable outcome, but after all it was a struggle between the Emperor of a moment and the King of endless ages, who had chosen for Himself the Crown of Thorns and deigned to allow the meanest of His subjects to don the royal insignia.

VIII

We must bring this chapter to a conclusion. But the student should realize all that our argument involves. For two hundred years the leaders among the Christians were branded as 'anarchists' and 'atheists', and hated accordingly. For two hundred years – we take a broad survey, qualifications and details have been pointed out, or will be dealt with later – to become a Christian meant the great renunciation, the joining a despised and persecuted sect, the swimming against the tide of popular prejudice, the coming under the ban of the Empire, the possibility at any moment of imprisonment and death under its most fearful forms. For two hundred years he that would follow Christ must count the cost, and be prepared to pay the same with his liberty and life. For two hundred years the mere profession of Christianity was itself a crime. *Christianus sum* was almost the one plea for which there was no forgiveness, in itself all that was necessary as a 'title' on the back of the condemned. He who made it was allowed neither to present apology nor to call in the aid of a pleader. 'Public hatred', writes Tertullian, 'asks but one thing, and that not investigation into the crimes charged, but simply the confession of the Christian Name.'

In the case of any other criminal, he continues, it is not enough that he declare himself to be a homicide, sacrilegious, incestuous, an enemy to the State. Before you give sentence, judges, you inquire vigorously into the circumstances, the nature of the deed, the time, place, and manner of its commission, the witnesses and accomplices. But in the trial of the Christians all this is dispensed with.

For the Name itself in periods of stress not a few meant the rack, the blazing shirt of pitch, the lion, the panther, or in the case of maidens an infamy worse than death.

Chapter Three

THE CAUSES OF HATRED

I

HITHERTO in our study of Persecution we have dealt with the relations of the Church and the Empire in their broadest outlines. We have seen that persecution was no accident, but the necessary resultant of certain main principles in Christianity itself, which brought the new faith into conflict with the outer world. We have also noted that the state of conflict was continuous, though persecution itself was intermittent. The fires of popular hatred were ever smouldering, liable at any moment to break out into sudden flame. A modern illustration will make our meaning clearer. The Jews in Russia are not always the victims of persecution, whether by the mob or the police. Periods, long or short, may elapse of comparative security, in which they suffer little save the curses and scowls of their neighbours. But ever and anon the fires blaze. So with the early Christians. They lived under the shadow of a great hate. We purpose in the present chapter to examine the reasons for this hate. We shall first point out two permanent causes of persecution apart from all political or social questions. The one was the ill-will of the Jews, the other the superstition of the heathen. We shall then inquire into the factors in the life or thought of the Church itself which brought upon it the suspicion and hatred of the world.

One caution at the outset may not be needless. For the economy of space, and that we may better grasp the broad outlines of our subject, we are driven to neglect, to some extent, the notes of time. But the student should not forget that persecution stretched over a period of two hundred and fifty years, and that during this period there were many changes not only in the Empire and other outer factors, but in the life of the Church. Nevertheless from the standpoint of the twentieth-century the period forms a unity in itself, in which for our immediate purpose we may neglect without great loss the details of internal change and development.

Judaism, in spite of its aggressive monotheism, had been recognized as a *religio licita* by the astute founder of the Empire, Julius Caesar, and endowed by himself and his successors with many privileges. Tiberius and Claudius, it is true, made efforts to check the growth of the Jews in Rome itself. But the attempt came too late, and ended in renewed and enlarged liberties. Not the least were the rights of civil jurisdiction over their own, especially in the East, constituting the Jews, as in the Middle Ages, a state within the State. With some reason the Jews claimed to be 'the second race' in the Empire. They alone, in spite of the outcries of literary swashbucklers and more sober historians, were exempt from offering sacrifices to the fortunes of Caesar and Rome, nor were they, as the conquered tribes, under the obligation of military service. To these franchises the destruction of Jerusalem made no difference; if anything, the loss of a local centre of intense nationalism and possible danger made concession the more easy.

The reader should beware lest he allow the fall of Jerusalem (Sept., 70) to lead him astray. Long before the Christian era the great centres of the Jewish race lay outside Palestine; Alexandria was of more importance than Jerusalem. Judaism in fact, under pressure from without, had slowly moulded itself into a non-sacrificial, non-sacerdotal religion, the bonds of which with the centre of the faith were rather sentimental than real. The synagogue and its ministry had become of more importance than the priest. The destruction of Jerusalem was the overthrow of a local sacrificial system, not the impairing of the real influence or spiritual vitality of Judaism. The power of the Dispersion, great before, was even increased by the abandonment of a centre whose intense and scornful conservatism had grown out of touch with the more progressive emigrant communities. We might even claim, without exaggeration, that the chief effect of the destruction of the Temple was the destruction not of Judaism, but of Jewish Christianity, the faith, that is, of St. James and the Church at Pella. Its influence on Judaism at large was not great: the substitution of a patriarch at Tiberias for the high-priest, of the schools of the rabbis for the struggling cliques at Jerusalem. Politically its effects were still less. In spite of growing hatred on the one side, and growing exclusiveness on the other, the Jewish religion continued to be privileged by the State, the Jews paying to the temple of Jupiter Capitolinus the two drachmae a head which they had hitherto paid to Jerusalem. The Jews were too invaluable for the finances of an Empire, impoverished by the excesses of Nero, to allow the Flavians and Antonines to yield to the outcries of the mob, or the scorn of their Juvenals.

The hatred felt for the Jews by the people at large, and the protection afforded them by the rulers for reasons of self-interest, form two of the most permanent features of history, as true in the first century as in the England of Henry II. Tales innumerable were told against them, full of poison and malice, but eagerly believed by all classes of society. They had been expelled from Egypt because of their leprosy. In their Holy of Holies was found an ass's head, a memorial, says Tacitus, of the salvation wrought for them, when dying of thirst in the wilderness, by a herd of wild asses who led them to the springs. Plutarch, however, rejects this idea; he is convinced that the Jews abstained from swine's flesh, because the pig was their god. After this we need not wonder that Juvenal sneers at the land where hogs never die except as the result of ripe old age, for swine's flesh is more precious there than human beings. But what can you expect, men argued, from a people who spend every seventh day in idleness, who despise Roman law and customs, who teach that they are never to point out the way except to those of their own faith, nor show the thirsty where to find a well, unless he is circumcised. At Alexandria, two of whose five districts were in the possession of the Jews, it was believed that they annually offered a Greek in sacrifice. Had it not been for the protection of the Roman officials, the Jews would have fared badly at the hands of the people. The police, it is true, generally came to their rescue, from motives of policy. But the real feeling of the Romans was one of utter contempt. 'O Marcomanni, O Quadi, O Sarmatians', cried Marcus Aurelius, on the completion of his journey through Palestine, 'at last I have found a race more lazy than you'. Every now and then, in spite of the police, the mob got the upper hand, slaughtered the Jews and burnt their houses. Of this hatred, at any rate in the earliest days, the Christians were the lineal heirs. But in their case the Roman protection was withdrawn.

Even more important was the hatred of the Jews for the Christians. As the synagogues, in the phrase of Tertullian, were 'the sources of persecution', it is important that we should realize the extent of the Jewish Dispersion. There were Jews in nearly every province of the Empire; but their numbers were greatest in Syria, Egypt, and Asia Minor. In Egypt, according to Philo, they totalled a million, or nearly one-sixth of the whole, figures presumably taken from the registers of taxation kept in that country. In Alexandria, where they governed themselves by means of a council (*gerusia*) and archons, they occupied at one time two out of the five quarters of a city of half a million inhabitants. In Syria, especially Antioch and Asia Minor, their numbers, though not the percentage, were even greater. 'The Jews,' said Philo, 'abound in every city of Asia and Syria.' Such was their influence at Apamea that at the beginning of the third century coins were struck by the city authorities with a figure and legend of Noah and his wife descending from the ark. In Rome, whence Tiberius transported four thousand able-bodied males to Sardinia (A.D. 19), they would number in the days of Claudius between ten and fifteen thousand in a city of a million. Here they were not organized into one great corporation as at Alexandria, but into a number of small private societies. Altogether the Jews formed seven per cent of the total population of the Empire, or at the least computation between four and five millions in all. Not without justice could Seneca complain:

> The customs of this notorious people have already come into such vogue that they have been introduced into every land; the conquered have given laws to the conquerors.

Mere numbers formed the least part of their influence. In some respects, though without a country, capital, or centre of worship, the Jews were the most homogeneous race in the Empire; if the most scattered, yet the most united; in the real elements of culture, second only to the Greeks; in wealth, then as now, the bankers of the world; strongest of all because of the rigid exclusiveness of their religion, a weapon more potent to guard their race than fortified frontiers. Nor must we underrate their social influence. In spite of the popular hatred, Judaism, owing to the decay of the old heathen faiths and the fascination of the Eastern cults, had attracted to itself proselytes and semi-proselytes in every land. These were not the less influential because both in motives and character they were curiously mixed, the eunuch of the Candace dynasty of Ethiopia side by side with the Empress Poppaea. In Rome Judaism became at one time a fashionable form of dilettanteism, circumcision included, until this last was stopped by the edicts of Hadrian and Septimius Severus. Nor was their power the less because it was massed in crowded ghettoes. Then, as now, the Jews refused to settle in the country. But Christianity also, whether because it originally grew up under the shadow of the synagogue, or from its Hellenic affinities, its lack of native missionaries, or other causes, was also at this period a town religion, which as yet had made little impression on the rural districts. Jews and Christians faced each other in the same cities, severed by a hatred that daily grew more intense. Not the least element in the persecution of the Christians would be the serious economic consequences which the Jews were able to inflict, especially upon those of their number who joined the Church.

The hatred, in the second century and afterwards, was not on the side of the Jew only. An intense hostility to everything Jewish is one of the marks of early Christian literature, most strongly emphasized perhaps in orthodox writings, in the *Epistle of Barnabas*. In this work, probably a picture of the intense antagonisms at Alexandria, the writer claims that all Jewish ceremonies are of the devil. Confronted with the difficulty what to make in this case of the Old Testament, he and his school boldly twisted it into a merely allegorical or spiritual narrative, which the Jews had misunderstood from the first. Others went further and maintained that the Old Testament from cover to cover had nothing to do with the Jews, who were but a synagogue of Satan. The heresy of Marcion, with its repudiation of the Old Testament along with Judaism, was but the logical expression of a widespread belief, of a hatred almost without parallel in history. From this heresy the Church was saved, not so much by the logic of its leaders – for the theology into which they were driven, to the twentieth century must seem more than questionable – as by its sense of historic spiritual continuity, that 'rock' upon which so much that is more valuable than logic is founded. Men realized that it was better to attempt, with St. Paul, to throw a bridge between the two, than, with Marcion of Pontus, to leave Christianity without historic (i.e. Jewish) foundations and supports. Even Tertullian, much as he detested Judaism, dreaded even more 'the Pontic mouse who nibbled away the Gospels'.

The hatred of Jew and Christian was the more bitter inasmuch as it thus partook of the nature of a family quarrel. As such it seems at first to have been regarded by the Romans, with a consequent indifference on their part to the real meaning of Christianity. This official indifference, of which we have many illustrations in the *Acts*, only stirred up the Jews the more vehemently to make the distinction between themselves and the Christians clear to their rulers. We have seen how the great fire of 64 gave them their opportunity. They succeeded once for all in convincing the police, who, according to a possible interpretation of a passage in Suetonius, had hitherto been in doubt on the subject, that the Christians were not members of the synagogues, and therefore not entitled to the political and religious franchises which enrolled members of the synagogues received. This distinction secured, the Jews lost no occasion of arousing against the Christians the political dread of the bureaucracy. The fall of Jerusalem and the later troubles of Judaism only added fresh fuel to the Jewish hatred. Said Justin Martyr, 'The Jews treat us as open enemies, putting us to death and torturing us, just as you heathens do, whenever they can.' Justin was speaking of the cruelty of the Jews to the Christians during 'their late war under Barcochba'. As a rule they were driven to more secret methods, the stirring up of the heathen mob, the scattering broadcast of horrible charges as to the Christians and their Saviour. In all persecutions, at any rate in Asia, we may detect the Jew in the background. We have illustrations of this in the cases of Polycarp and Pionius. To the Jew also the Roman governor was generally indebted for the distorted impression he formed of the religion of the prisoner before him. Said the prefect Epolius to Conon, an old gardener upon an imperial estate in Pamphylia, of whom we shall hear again:

> Why are you such a fool as to call a man God, and that, too, one who died a violent death? For so have I learnt accurately from the Jews, both as to his race and his manifestations to their nation, and his death by crucifixion. They brought his memoirs, and read them out to me. Leave off this folly, and enjoy life along with us.

As Eusebius informs us:

> Their apostles, conveying formal letters ... (for the Jews give the name of 'apostle' to those who convey encyclical epistles from their rulers) swarmed everywhere on earth, calumniating the gospel of our Saviour –

spreading abroad also infamous tales about the Christians, destined in later ages to return in awful retribution on their own head.

The hatred of the Jews was especially felt by the Jewish Christians. This Church, the original Church of Christendom, to which at one time all the Apostles belonged with the exception of St. Paul, split up even during the lifetime of St. James into two sections. The one section, led by St. Peter and St. John, recognized the logic of accomplished facts, and remembered the words of Jesus concerning the guidance of the Spirit. After a period of hesitation, which filled St. Paul with indignation, St. Peter, as we see from his Epistle, and as his death at Rome conclusively proves, ceased to be a 'Jewish Christian', and became one with the Gentile Church. But the party, known later as Nazarenes, survived his defection. The other section, at a later date called the Ebionites, refused to own the Gentile Church as the true Church, and after doing all they could in his lifetime to thwart St. Paul, tried to discredit his memory after death. With a fidelity worthy of a better cause, both sections clung to their Judaism, even after the destruction of the Temple had destroyed their basis of existence. So they fell between two fires. On the one hand they were despised by the Church. Jerome, who knew them well, contemptuously but accurately describes them as 'semi-Jews' and 'semi-Christians'. As such the Church in time put them on her roll of heretics; an astonishing but deserved result for a Church, undoubtedly primitive and apostolic, but which refused to recognize the laws of growth and development; in other words, could not discern the mission of the Holy Ghost. On the other hand they were pursued with especial hatred;

> not merely at the hands of Jewish children, but, rising at dawn, at noon, at eventide, when they perform their orisons in the synagogues, the Jews curse them and anathematize them, saying, 'God curse the Nazarenes'. ... They are Jews more than anything else, and yet they are detested by the Jews.

So this band of irreconcileables lingered on, first at Pella, then afterwards amid the ruins of Jerusalem, until driven away from the new city of Aelia Capitalina, founded by Hadrian on the site of the Holy City. It would not tend to peace between the two branches of Christendom that while no Jew was allowed to approach the city under pain of death, a prohibition which Jewish Christians, we imagine, would apply to themselves, other Christians, Gentiles in origin, made the new Jerusalem the seat of a bishopric under the Gentile Marcus. As with other similar movements that mark arrested development, these Jewish Christians but slowly decayed. They still survive, it would seem, in Mesopotamia, in a hopelessly corrupt condition. Their history, for the most part a blank, is that of a rudimentary organ in the Church, a perpetual warning of the atrophy which attends unreasoning subservience to the dead hand. Their record – throughout their early existence under the control of 'the relatives of our Lord' – shows the value of the decision of St. Paul, that henceforth he would not know Christ after the flesh (2 Cor. 5: 16).

But whatever their record theologically, the 'relatives' of Jesus did not shrink from suffering for their faith. The death of St. James, their leader, was for them the beginning of persecution. Eusebius tells us that 'after the martyrdom of St. James' the disciples at Jerusalem, led by 'those related to our Lord,' elected 'His paternal uncle's son, Symeon the son of Clopas, the cousin-german of Jesus,' to be the second bishop. A few years later Vespasian 'commanded all of the family of David to be sought after, that no one might be left among the Jews of the royal stock.' Symeon and his brethren survived this persecution, evidently political rather than religious in character. We may find the reason in a story, told at a later date, of two grandsons of St. Jude, the brother of Jesus. Domitian, for reasons similar to those of his father Vespasian, had renewed the persecution of the 'the descendants of David'. Whereupon 'the heretics accused the grandsons of Jude'. When they were brought before the emperor,

Domitian demanded whether they were of the stock of David? This being confessed, he asked again: What possession and what substance they had. They answered that they had no more between them but nine and thirty acres of land, and that they sustained their families by their own labour; showing forth their hands to the emperor, being hard and rough, and worn with labours, to witness that the words they had spoken were true. . . . So Domitian, despising them as vile persons, let them go.

After this release 'they ruled the Church as witnesses (μάρτυρες) and as relatives of the Lord.' But at a later date Symeon, if we may trust Hegesippus, was crucified as a Christian 'after he had been tortured for several days'.

The last relative of Jesus of whom we have knowledge died as a martyr, probably under Decius, on the accusation, as it would appear, of the Jews. Conon, the gardener of Magydus, on being asked by the governor Epolius the usual preliminary questions, declared:

'I came from the town of Nazareth in Galilee, and am a kinsman of Christ.' 'If you know Christ,' replied the tyrant, 'know our gods also. Be persuaded by me and, by all the gods, you shall gain great honours. I don't say "Sacrifice," or anything of that sort. It will be enough to take a pinch of incense, a drop of wine and an olive branch, and say: "Most sovereign Zeus, save this multitude!" '

But Conon was true to his royal lineage, one only of many hundreds of Christians throughout the Empire who suffered death by reason of the hatred of the Jews.

II

Not less universal as a factor in the persecution of the Christians was the superstition of the heathen. This affected the Church in two ways; the one familiar to us from frequent references in the apologists; the other closely connected with the first, the widespread belief in the practice by the Christians of the magic arts. But upon this second the Christian apologists do not dwell.

For their old religion, in the higher sense of the word, the Romans in the second century had little concern. They sought the satisfaction of their spiritual longings in devotion to some exotic cult, or in the pursuit of the Stoic and Platonic philosophies. But the governing classes still attached importance to religion as a branch of the civil service primarily concerned with the safety of the State. Its observance was the duty of every citizen, and was even a more necessary part of patriotism than service in the army, because the sin of a single recusant might call down the anger of the neglected gods on the whole state. This last in fact was the very thing that in the judgement of popular superstition occurred. Flood, earthquake, and pestilence were all of them traced to the offended gods, who had thus visited upon the people the neglect and sacrilege of the Christians. 'If', writes Tertullian,

the Tiber floods the City, or the Nile refuses to rise, or the sky withholds its rain, if there is an earthquake, famine, or pestilence, at once the cry is raised: Christians to the lions.

In North Africa the practice passed into a proverb: 'If there is no rain, lay the blame on the Christians'.

The superstition of the heathen further charged the Christians with the practice of magic arts. In this matter it is important that we should be fair. The blame must not be thrown altogether upon the heathen. Thoughout the Empire the Jews were known as exorcists. The belief in the magic of Solomon is no invention of the Arabian Nights; we find it well established in the days of Josephus. The Christians probably believed in magic every whit as heartily as the heathen; nor would they have been backward in claiming for their leaders the possession of supernatural powers. The diffidence in this matter of a Church familiarized with the arguments of Hume or Huxley never dawned upon them. In the study of history we must beware above all of mental anachronism. To approach the subject of the charge of magic with modern prepossessions is fatal. In fact, the charge against the Christians of using the black arts was to some extent the result of their own claims. These claims we may explain as we will. For the historian explanation or lack of explanation is immaterial. For him a belief, however erroneous, if widely held, is a factor in human life and progress which he dare not ignore.

In the second and third centuries superstition was, if anything, a growing force. The old Latin farmer was superstitious enough, but his superstitions were rather nature-dreads, fears, such as ever haunt the illiterate, of the vast forces of the world around him. These he tried to propitiate in diverse ways. But the later Roman, for whom an age of conquest and travel had robbed the solitude of forest and sea of much of their awe, had fled to religions, whose mysticism, such as it was, was largely founded upon spiritual horror. From the Emperor on the throne to the meanest slave, men trembled at the awful powers of the unknown, and trembled the more because of their loss of religious faith. They peopled the heaven and earth with a host of demons – daemons the philosophers vainly called them – and believed with all their hearts in the alliance of magicians and sorcerers with the hordes of the black one. Dreams and omens haunted high and low alike. We see this in the popular treatise on their interpretation published at the close of the second century by Artemidorus, a work full of the wildest and most superstitious hallucinations. The curious student who turns over its pages will find 'besotted credulity disguising itself under the forms of scientific inquiry.' Spiritualism, with all its paraphernalia of table-rapping, writing by invisible hands, clairvoyance, and the like, became the fashion, and assisted in seducing Julian the Apostate from Christianity. Sludge the Medium has his prototype in Alexander of Abonutichos, or the earlier Simon Magus. For the more devout there were the mysteries of Isis and Mithra, with their beliefs in the tyranny of the stars over human lives. From his youth Tiberius was the slave of astrologists.

Domitian lived in perpetual fear of the fulfilment of Chaldean prophecies, while Marcus Aurelius surrounded himself with Egyptian magicians.

In their belief in demons and other supernatural agencies the Christians were not before their age, save in their grasp of the supremacy of one benign Father of good. Behind every idol statue, however beautiful, they discerned the grinning face of a fiend. The devil and his angels were terrible realities, whose evil machinations were only thwarted by the ceaseless vigilance of the attendant spirits of good. As in the romance of Enoch, archangels and demons struggled for the soul and body, nor was the struggle one-sided. For the demons 'fill the atmosphere which extends between earth and heaven'. Owing to their speed they are almost omniscient, and thus 'attain credit for causing that which they announce'. For the Christian the miraculous was so common that it ceased to be miraculous. For him, as for the pagan, it formed part of the ordinary machinery of the universe. Illustrations of this belief are almost co-extensive with the literature of the early and mediaeval Church. Two examples must suffice, by no means either extraordinary or peculiar. St. Augustine, whom no one can accuse of either insincerity or stupidity, solemnly asserts that in his own diocese of Hippo, in the space of two years there had occurred no less than seventy-two miracles, among them five cases of restoration to life.

The works of Sulpicius Severus bear the marks of a cultured mind of singular sincerity. His Life of St. Martin of Tours, one of the gems of Christian biography, is the record of an eye-witness, yet marred with the grossest tales of the miraculous. He begins by imploring his readers

to give full faith to my statements, and not to believe that I have written anything of which I have not certain knowledge and proof, for I should have preferred to have kept silence rather than relate the false.

'Martin,' he claims elsewhere, 'does not need to be defended by untruths.' Yet in one place he tells us how St. Martin restored three dead men to life, and twits Egyptian monks, for whom otherwise he has a profound reverence, with their inability to perform this feat.

With this brief statement of the Christian position, a matter which might well claim a volume for its adequate exposition, the reader will the better understand how the heathen came to associate their name with the black arts. So far as demons were concerned, the Church professed that it was part of its mission to fight them, as, in fact, it had been part of the work of Jesus on earth. For the Christian,

> The ancient Prince of ill,
> Look grim as e'er he will,

is absolutely the most futile of beings. 'Thou art utterly despicable,' said St. Anthony, one of the great, if shadowy types of the early Church, to the demon that cowered at his feet; 'thou art black of soul, yet weak as a child. Henceforth I will not cast one thought on thee.' In this consciousness of victory over the powers of evil lay one secret of the success of the Church. Devils existed – that was undeniable, accepted by heathen and Christian alike. But the Christians claimed that they possessed the means of subduing them.

I will not argue the matter any further, writes Tertullian. There is a quicker way of demonstrating the truth. Let a demoniac, acknowledged as such, be brought before your tribunal. Then let that spirit be commanded to speak by any Christian, and he will profess himself a devil as sincerely as elsewhere he falsely asserts that he is a god.

And the conquered devils, adds Minucius Felix, because of their fears, stir up against the Christians persecution and hatred. One early order in the Church, the exorcists, was specially dedicated to the task. They cast out devils, so the Church believed, by the use of the name of Jesus, and by the sign or mention of the Cross. Their superior powers in this matter – for the Christians acknowledged some reality in heathen enchantments – were acknowledged by the heathen, and were twisted against them, for instance, by Celsus, as they had been twisted by the scribes against our Lord, into a proof of alliance with the demons themselves. Undoubtedly they were sorcerers, their successes showed that, of whom Jesus with His 'miracles' had been the master and leader.

Of the widespread belief in the second and third centuries in the magic arts of the Christians the proofs are overwhelming. 'Where are the magicians, your teachers in this jugglery?' said Marcian to the martyr Achatius. Some have found evidence of this suspicion in the earliest times in the punishment devised for the Christians by Nero. By Roman law, those condemned for abetting magical practices were condemned to be thrown to the beasts, or to be crucified, while actual sorcerers were to be burnt alive. Nero confused these punishments together, by condemning the Christians to be wrapped in the skins of beasts and thus exposed to savage dogs, or to be smeared with pitch, then fastened to crosses, and set on fire. Probably, in our judgement, the punishment was rather the coincidence of cruelty than a judicial sentence. But if Nero had lived in a later age we should have decided otherwise, not merely because of heathen opinion, but also by reason of the magical or semi-magical beliefs which had invaded the Church itself, and which still, alas! in some quarters retain their ancient power. Cyprian tells us stories of the supernatural powers of the consecrated elements worthy of that great master of mediaeval superstition, Caesar of Heisterbach; while Gregory the Wonder-worker (Thaumaturgus), deliberately adopted credulity as one of the auxiliaries of the Church in the conversion of the heathen. The Christians of the third century had largely themselves to thank if they were looked upon as too familiar with the black art.

The effect of all this on the persecution of the Christians needs but little explanation. To the dire magic of the Christians were attributed not only the disasters of nature, but the failure of the current religion. The heathen believed that by their superior exorcisms the Christians could reduce to silence oracles which hitherto had proved the fortune of a whole country; that in many ways their black arts caused the customary manifestations of the supernatural to miscarry. According to Dionysius of Alexandria, it was this that led to the outbreak of the Valerian persecution:

Never was there any of the emperors before him so favourably and benevolently disposed towards the Christians. . . . His palace was indeed an ecclesia of the Lord. But the chief of the Egyptian magi persuaded him to abandon this course, exhorting him to slay these holy men as enemies and obstacles to their detestable incantations. For there were and still are among the Christians many whose mere presence and look, though they merely breathed and spoke, are able to put to nought the artifices of wicked demons.

We have an interesting illustration, both of the current superstition and its relation to the persecution of the Christians, in the career of the impostor Alexander of Abonutichos, as described for us by the master-hand of Lucian. Acting on the credulity of the 'fat-head' Paphlagonians, Alexander, 'a fine, handsome man with a real touch of divinity about him,' set up in his native town of Abonutichos an oracle of Aesculapius. Lucian describes minutely how the trick was done. Brazen tablets were buried in the temple of Apollo at Chalcedon, announcing that Aesculapius would shortly pay a visit to Pontus. The 'chewing of soap-wort', a 'serpent's head of linen', and the 'burying of a goose-egg in which he had inserted a new-born reptile,' did the rest. The clever rascal – 'who never made a small plan, his ideas were always large' – after proper formalities, dug up the buried egg, 'and announced that here he held Aesculapius'. When the crowd saw the reptile, 'they raised a shout, hailed the God, blessed the city, and every mouth was full of prayers.' Bithynia and Galatia flocked to see the new-born deity.

Alexander proclaimed that on a stated day the god would give answers to all comers. Each person was to write down his wish and the object of his curiosity, fasten the packet with thread, seal it with wax. Alexander would receive these . . . and return the packets with the seals intact and the answers attached.

Lucian adds, for the information of the unskilled in these matters, three methods by which the seals could be opened and refastened. As for his oracles, 'some were crabbed and ambiguous, others unintelligible.' Of the latter, the following may serve: 'Morphi ebargulis for night Chnenchiorante shall leave the light.' But unintelligible or ambiguous, the trick succeeded. At a fixed charge of a shilling per oracle, Alexander made something like £3,000 a year. His agents were everywhere, spreading abroad, on commission, the fame of the new god. 'At Rome the only question was who should be the first to fly to Abonutichos.' We must not prolong the astonishing story. But it is of importance to note that when Alexander was

instituting his mysteries with hierophants and torchbearers complete ... on the first day proclamation was made to this effect: If there be any atheist or Christian or Epicurean here spying upon our rites, let him depart in haste ... Alexander himself led the litany with the cry, 'Christians, begone.'

The crowd responded; for the evil eye of the Christians, to say nothing of their sorceries, could ruin even an oracle of Aesculapius.

Another interesting illustration is the story of the five sculptors of Sirmium. At one of Diocletian's quarries in Pannonia there was an encampment of 622 masons and carvers, under a number of 'philosophers', or foremen. Among them there were four Christians of special ability who won the praise of Diocletian by quarrying a single block of stone, out of which they carved a group twenty-five feet in length. One of the gang, Simplicius, found that his tools broke more frequently than those of his comrades. He asked the reason, and was told by his companions that it was because they were Christians. He thereupon requested his friends to bless his tools also, and was so impressed by the good results that he too became a disciple, and was baptized by Bishop Cyril of Antioch, who for three years had been a slave in the quarries. The little band soon fell into trouble, through the jealousy of their pagan comrades. One of the 'philosophers' observed them making the sign of the cross upon all their works. A few months later Diocletian ordered the four to carve an image of Aesculapius. The Christians, who had carved without demur an image of the sun, refused to touch that of the hated rival 'saviour'. The 'philosophers' saw their opportunity, and accused the stonemasons of Christianity and magic. Diocletian was vexed. 'I will not have my skilled workmen reviled,' he said. But after some delay his hatred of Christianity prevailed over his love of good artists. He ordered them to be beaten with scorpions, then enclosed in lead and thrown into the river Save.

III

Hitherto we have considered the causes of hatred that in some degree might be considered as external to Christianity, discordant or antagonistic factors in its environment. We now turn to the elements in the life and faith of the Early Church which brought against it the charge of anarchism, and the wrath of both mob and empire. The study of these will throw light, not only upon the origin of persecution, but also upon the thought and character of the Church of the early Fathers. One caution must be given at the outset. Persecution as a rule did not affect the average member of the Church; it fell hardly upon the extremists, the out-and-outs, call them what we will. The elements in Christian life upon which we shall dwell in the sections of this chapter must not, therefore, be taken to be of necessity the characteristics of the ordinary member. But earthly institutions should not be judged by their averages, but by the ideals of their leaders.

There were in the main five internal causes of the hatred felt for the Church by government and people. First, though not foremost in importance, was the effect of Christianity as a disintegrating factor upon the *familia* – a word not adequately represented by the modern 'family' – including the tendency among many of the early Christians to discourage marriage. In the eyes of St. Paul, this last was part of the renunciation laid upon him by the Lord Jesus, and though he is careful not to elevate this individual rule into a law for all, nevertheless there can be little doubt of the general impression that his defence of celibacy produced. Even in the cases where marriages were allowed, inter-marriage with heathen was forbidden; a command necessary indeed if the purity of the Christian faith should be maintained. The effect, however, must have been constant friction with heathen families, who would bitterly resent what they would regard as the Christian pride and aloofness. They would feel, not without justice, that the Christians despised the world in which they lived, and were somewhat contemptuous of its race interests and family bonds. 'Tampering with domestic relations' was one of the earliest charges brought against the followers of Jesus. This belief in Christian misanthropy would be strengthened by the incautious quotation before the heathen of the many hard sayings of the Saviour, especially those dealing with the family. For Jesus had owned that He

came not to send peace, but a sword. For I am come to set a man at variance against his father, and the daughter against her mother, and the daughter-in-law against her mother-in-law. And a man's foes shall be they of his own household. Matt. 10: 34–5.

All this was inevitable, and needs neither explanation nor illustrations. Variance in the home is the first effect of missionary effort, whether in the second or the twentieth century. One example must suffice for many, the case of Alce of Smyrna, whom Ignatius calls 'that name beloved by me.' Her brother Herod, the eirenarch or chief of the police, and her father Nicetas were foremost in securing the condemnation of Polycarp.

The student, moreover, should remember that the pagan world would not distinguish, with the care of his text-books, between the heretical and Catholic views. Heretical anti-social views abounded, and would add to the uneasiness of the governing classes. For the Roman, in spite of growing luxury and licence, still looked upon the family as the unit-cell of the State and the foundation of morality. If the *Acts of St. Paul and Thekla* had fallen into the hands of an intelligent Roman official, could we have blamed him if he had detected its dangerous tendencies? Here is a document, he would have argued, dealing with one of the leaders of this sect, in which we see that the first effect of the preaching of St. Paul is for Thekla to refuse as sinful the marriage arranged for her by her parents:

Whereupon her betrothed went out into the street and kept a watch upon those who went in and out to Paul. And he saw two men bitterly contending with each other. 'Men,' he said, 'who are you? and who is that fellow with you in the house who leads astray the souls of young men and deceives virgins so that they refuse to marry, but remain as they are?' And Demas answered him: 'Who this is we do not know, but he deprives young men of wives and maidens of husbands by saying that in no other way shall there be a resurrection for you save by remaining chaste and keeping the flesh chaste.'

Nor would our Roman official have been favourably impressed by the rest of the story, how Thekla bribed the gaoler with her bracelets that she might gain access by night to the Apostle, how on escape from prison Thekla ran after St. Paul and said, 'I will cut off my hair and follow thee whithersoever thou goest,' and much else to the same effect.

The *Acts of Paul and Thekla* is a second-century romance written by a Syrian presbyter, the historical basis of which it is difficult to dissever from its later accretions. But the romance for our present purpose is a real document, for the tale was accepted by the Church with enthusiastic belief. We may instance, moreover, as confirmation of the same tendency in certain sections of the Church, the examination in the time of Diocletian of Pollio, a 'reader' of Cibalae (Vinkovce), a town in Hungary.

'What is your name?' asked the judge. 'Pollio.' 'Are you a Christian?' 'Yes.' 'What office do you hold?' 'I am chief of the readers.' 'What do you mean by a reader?' 'One whose duty it is to read God's word to the congregation.' 'You mean those people who impose upon silly women (*mulierculas*) and tell them that they must not marry, and persuade them to adopt a fanciful chastity.'

Le Blant has pointed out another way in which, in certain extreme sections, Christianity would run counter to the Roman ideas of the family. In Gaul, it seems, Christian inscriptions rarely mention parentage. Acting on a mistaken interpretation of the words of Jesus, the Christians of Gaul refused to call any man father. We have illustrations of this of an earlier date. 'Of what parents are you born?' said the judge to Lucian of Antioch. 'I am a Christian,' he answered, 'and a Christian's only relatives are the saints.'

Moreover, with the best intentions in the world, and under the most judicious missionaries, the proselytizing efforts of the Christians, by thrusting a wedge into the life of the home, could not fail at times to give rise to scandals. We see this in the case of Dativus, a decurion or senator of Carthage, who, on the defection of its bishop, had shepherded the Church of Abitini. Forty-nine of the little flock were brought to Carthage and tried. When Dativus was stretched on the hobby horse, a charge was laid against him by a certain Fortunatianus, a noble barrister of Carthage,

'that in the absence of our father, and while I was at my studies, he seduced our sister Victoria and led her and two other girls away from this great city of Abitini. In fact, he never entered our house without beguiling the girls' minds with his soft soap.' Victoria interrupted with a Christian's freedom of speech: 'I set out and journeyed to Abitini of my own free will, and not at the persuasion or in the company of Dativus. I can call citizens to prove this.'

Dativus would not be alone in such charges. We may be sure that the heathen interpreted the most innocent acts into occasions of scandal. Thus we read, during the persecution of Diocletian, of several Christian girls from Thessalonica, who ran off to the mountains without their father's knowledge. By the sentence he passed upon Irene, their leader, the judge Dulcetius evidently considered that they were women of frail reputation.

Or turn to the misunderstandings and persecutions to which Christians were exposed in the home itself. The Roman *familia* was scarcely the modern English family; it was a little world of its own, the head of which had autocratic powers jealously guarded by the law from autocratic interference. The result, as in modern India, was inevitable. Unfortunately, we possess no records giving us an account in any detail of the experiences of a convert in a heathen home of the old world. Lanciani has published an inscription of the second century written on the tomb of a daughter of whom the father says: 'She was a pagan among pagans, a believer among believers.' Between the lines we can read much; the child of a mixed marriage doing her best to live in peace in a home where the father was a heathen, the mother a Christian. Justin Martyr also tells a tale, in many of its details, probably, characteristic of the times. A woman after her conversion sought to purify her own life and that of her licentious husband. Finding this last to be impossible, she determined to separate from him, and sought a divorce. In revenge the husband denounced his wife and her 'teacher', Ptolemy, as Christians. Ptolemy was 'questioned on this sole point', and on his confession was led away to death. The wife, however, escaped, by the subtlety of her lawyers. They persuaded her to appeal to the emperor for time 'to settle her affairs', before making answer on this capital charge. This was granted. But such a settlement involved the restoration by the spendthrift husband of the dowry of his wife. As the husband could not find the money, he took care not to present himself in court. In the absence of accuser the charge fell to the ground, in accordance with the decision of Hadrian.

For the Christian wife, conflict with her heathen husband would be accentuated by the arrival of the first baby. No woman who had worshipped the Child of Bethlehem could ever allow to go unchallenged the *patria potestas*, the right of the father to decide which of his children should be permitted to live, and which should be cast into the street, or exposed on the Island in the Tiber. 'If it proves a girl,' writes a father in Alexandria to his expectant wife, 'throw it out.' As to this and other evil practices sanctioned by a home-life in many respects elevated and pure the issue was clear. But our sympathies are less assured in other matters, for instance, Tertullian's portrait of a Christian wife who has at her side a servant of the devil – this is his pleasant name for her husband. The man, he says, is sure to be such a brute that if it is a fast day he will 'arrange to hold a feast the same day'. He will further prove his allegiance to Satan by taking it ill that his wife

for the sake of visiting the brethren goes round from street to street to other men's cottages, especially those of the poor. . . . He will not allow her to be absent all night long at nocturnal convocations and paschal solemnities . . . or suffer to creep into prison to kiss a martyr's bonds, or even to exchange a kiss with one of the brethren.

After this it is a little matter that her signing 'her bed and her body with the Cross' will arouse his suspicions. If the fellow endures his wife and her ways at all it will simply be because of her dowry, or that he may make her his slave by his threats of dragging her before the executioner. We can hardly believe that all pagan husbands were brutes, or all Christian wives so lacking at times in discretion. But, at the best, the situation in a mixed marriage was difficult, almost impossible, as Tertullian, in spite of his extravagance, rightly saw.

The difficulties of the Christian in a pagan home did not cease with his death. Should he be buried with pagan rites and inscriptions, amid his pagan relatives, or should he lie apart? The matter of the inscription was not of much importance; it was not well for the Christian to advertise his religion too prominently on his tomb. Many, in fact, inserted the customary pagan formula D.M. (*Dis Manibus*), probably without clear idea of its meaning. In many cases the epitaphs and signs are ambiguous. But the question of the separate tomb is of more moment. The early Christians rightly laid stress on burial among the brethren. This however, involved the exclusion of pagans. Hence husbands lie apart from their wives, children from their parents. In one case permission is actually given in an epitaph for two husbands to be buried with their wives, provided they become converts.

As regards one cause of offence the heathen certainly had justice on their side. In 220 Callistus, who had risen from a slave to be the pope, unfortunately declared that henceforth the Church would sanction that a girl of high position should give her hand to a freedman, careless of the fact that such a union could not possibly be a legal marriage. The plea of Callistus, that Christian girls of noble rank far outnumbered young men in the Church of the same position – 'a rich unmarried man in the house of God it is difficult to find', owns Tertullian – can hardly justify this daring defiance of public opinion. Its effect, all questions of morality apart, was to open the door to the many abuses of an ecclesiastical as distinct from a civil law of marriage. In matters like these we see some of the reasons for the dislike and persecution of the Church.

IV

We pass on to the consideration of two minor causes of heathen hatred. As regards both the student should beware of exaggeration. But in some quarters they would have importance.

The first of these was the Christian conception of property. We do not allude to the communism which at first prevailed at Jerusalem. Too much importance has been attached to an experiment, soon abandoned, at no time so completely developed as among the Jewish sects of Essenes and Therepeutae. Communism in the Church, under the guise of Monasticism, did not become a power until the age of persecution was past. Nor do we refer to the hostility of vested interests, though undoubtedly at all times this would be a serious factor. We allude rather to the completely altered conception that Christianity must have effected in its disciples as regards property in slaves. No doubt Harnack is right when he claims that no 'slave question' in the modern sense of the word occupied the early Church. In the Kingdom of God, as in the realm of nature, slow development is the law of life. In the case of an institution so interwoven with the whole social fabric as was slavery this was inevitable. Though in his Epistle to Philemon the word emancipation is always trembling on the lips of St. Paul, he never quite utters it, while it took the Church centuries to rise to the noble ideal of the great Apostle. Christians throughout the era of persecution held slaves, as other men, and as the Jews had done before them, and were troubled by no stings of conscience. But every Christian who knew anything of the religion he professed must have recognized that with Jesus legal rights are strictly limited by the higher law of love. The code, for instance, refused to recognize the marriage of slaves; the Christian master could not content himself with mere cohabitation (*contubernium*), unblessed by the Church, dissoluable at will. Slavery might be necessary; nevertheless, pleads Clement of Alexandria, 'slaves are men like ourselves', to whom the Golden Rule applies. To the same effect was the reply of Lactantius to those who pointed out that the Christians possessed slaves: 'Slaves are not slaves to us. We deem them brothers after the spirit, in religion fellow-servants.' A confirmation of this may be found in the fact pointed out by de Rossi that the inscription 'slave' is never met with in the catacombs, though nothing is more common on the tombs of heathen.

Moreover, from the first the Church claimed to ordain slaves as deacons, priests, and bishops, a revolution, silent, unheralded, the full effect of which it is difficult to exaggerate. Hitherto a slave had been a thing, scarcely human. 'Implements', writes Varro, 'are of three kinds; vocal, including slaves, semi-vocal, e.g. oxen, and dumb, for instance ploughs.' Now, in the language of a growing sacerdotalism, this 'implement', that could be bought on the market for less than £20, could become the successor of the Apostles, or, in the words of Ignatius, the representative of the Lord Himself. That Callistus, Bishop of Rome, had been a slave, whatever be the truth, or otherwise, as to his faults, marks a new era in the history of humanity not without its parallel in the case of Epictetus the slave-apostle of Stoicism. But this higher law of love, this conception of the slave not only as a brother in Christ Jesus, who sat side by side at the same agapé, or partook of the same loaf and cup at the Lord's Supper, but as a leader in the Church, responsible to God for the souls of his flock, could hardly fail to arouse suspicion and mis-understanding. Roman governors, conscious of the vast slave populations, were ever anxious lest there should be a servile outbreak. Heathen leg-atees would scarcely view with approval a *familia* which they found leavened through and through with the freedom of Christ. In a few instances also the new doctrines might lead to the alterations of wills, and the bequeathing of slaves out of the family to members of the same Church. In any case the master, of whom Tertullian tells us, who, direct-ly that he heard that his slave had become a Christian, sent him to the dreaded *ergastulum*, or slaves' work-prison, would not be alone in his fear or cruelty.

Nor can there be reasonable doubt that the early Church, apart al-together from questions of slavery, was saturated through and through with Ebionite conceptions. In some writers poverty was as much the essential mark of the Christian as it afterwards became of the spiritual Franciscans. Wealth was one of the things of the world which it was the Christian's business to renounce, though, alas, complete renunciation could only be achieved by the few. For the higher orders of the ministry, however, poverty was considered absolutely essential. All this would lend colour to the charge of anarchism under which, as we have seen, the Christians were condemned.

A further cause of suspicion, not, it is true, of much importance, would be found in the views of many Christians as to the fate of the world, including their neighbours. The Church in the second century believed that the world lay in the grip of the Evil One, and that it was fast hastening to its doom of 'blood and fire'. The Christian watchword was still, as in the first century, Maran Atha, 'the Lord is at hand'. Their wandering 'prophets' – an order in the Church which died out after the second century, to reappear in sundry forms in modern Nonconformity – made this time, in especial, the basis of their sermons. Many seem to have gloried (at least that was the impression produced upon the heathen) in the retribution so speedily to come upon the world. No doubt some of their utterances – illustrations may be found in the Chris-tian *Sibylline Oracles* – were as indiscreet as have been the utterances on this matter of fanatics in later ages. Celsus, for instance, naturally com-plains of the—

many who roam like tramps through cities and camps ... and commit to everlasting fire cities and lands and their inhabitants ... mixing up their mighty threats with half-crazy and perfectly senseless words, which every fool applies to suit his own purpose.

Impostors, from whom the Church in every century has suffered many things, were foremost, as was natural, in these exaggerations and half-truths. We see this in the case of Proteus Peregrinus, who seems to have passed as a 'prophet'. By these impostors, too often beggars in disguise, would the Church be judged by outsiders, as it was by Lucian and Celsus.

The effect of this preaching of retribution by means of terrific images regarded as actual realities would vary with different classes. The cultured, whose idea was that of Vergil: 'Happy the man who has placed beneath his feet fears and inexorable fate and the roar of greedy Hell,' would look on it with loathing as a return to those horrors of superstition from which Lucretius had sought to deliver mankind by means of his great sceptical poem. 'The Crucified', they said, 'repels all gladness' – 'Tantum religio potuit suadere malorum'. The followers of Epicurus, with their profound belief in a morningless and unawakening sleep, would disdain teacher and teaching alike. Said Tertullian:

'We get ourselves laughed at for proclaiming that God will one day judge the world, though, like us, poets and philosophers set up a judgement-seat in the world below. And if we threaten Gehenna, a reservoir of secret fire under the earth for purposes of punishment, we have derision heaped upon us' (*Apol.* 47).

To the vulgar the dread of Tartarus, 'with its vistas of rivers of fire and stygian cliffs . . . of spectres mowing at us with terrible faces', was still a living reality; and the preaching of the Christians was not without its results. But, broadly speaking, the gloomy Millenarianism of much second-century Christianity could not fail to arouse hatred and suspicion. Nor would it lessen the offence that the doom of the heathen would usher in the reign of the saints, 'the coming age in which the elect of God shall dwell'.

V

A more important cause of popular hatred lay in the misunderstanding of the nature of certain Christian rites and ceremonies. 'The conviction,' writes Mommsen,

that the Christian conventicles were orgies of lewdness, and receptacles of every crime, got hold on the popular mind with all the terrible vehemence of an aversion that resists all arguments and heeds not refutation.

In part these charges were due to Christian secrecy, a necessary result of the aloofness or renunciation which underlay their faith. Of this secrecy or aloofness, and the jealousy with which it was guarded, we have an extreme instance, if Chrysostom is to be trusted, in the case of Babylas of Antioch, who endured martyrdom rather than allow the Emperor Decius to intrude upon the privacy of his congregation. We need not be surprised at the result. That which is secret, as Caecilius pointed out to Minucius Felix, always lies under the suspicion of being the abominable. In part, also, the charges were due to the misunderstanding or distortion of Christian phrases. The 'kiss of peace' which St. Paul had instituted, and which long continued a factor in the life of the Western Church, both lent itself to licentious interpretations, and, as Clement of Alexandria owns, was put to wrong uses by some who 'do nothing but make the Church resound with their kisses'. 'See how these Christians love one another' may have been originally the sarcasm of impure minds upon these 'unholy kisses, full of poison, counterfeiting sanctity', wrested by Tertullian to a nobler use. The evening agapés – the title itself was suspicious – were twisted into scenes of unbridled lust, at which 'the dogs, our friends forsooth! overturn the lamps, and obtain for us the shamelessness of darkness'. 'Three things,' writes Athenagoras, 'are alleged against us: Atheism, Thyestean feasts, Oedipodean intercourse' – in other words, cannibalism and incest – 'If these things are true, spare none of us.' And because the people thought they were true they spared but few when the fury seized them.

The charge of cannibalism was the result of misunderstanding of the Christian Sacraments. The carrying of infants to the house of prayer to obtain Baptism was twisted, as in the case of the Jews in the Middle Ages, into a horrible design, mixed up in popular imagination with the Eucharist, the bread of which was supposed to be used 'to collect the gushing blood' of the babes. For us the language of the Lord's Supper, hallowed by nineteen hundred years of association, has lost its original and startling daring. 'Except ye eat My flesh and drink My blood, ye have no life in yourselves' would sound more than strange to heathen ears. To Porphyry, by no means an unfair critic, it seemed

trivial and absurd, surpassing all absurdity and trivial coarseness, for a man to eat human flesh and drink the blood of his fellow-tribesman or relative, and thereby win eternal life. Tell me what greater coarseness could you introduce into life, if you practise that habit? What crime will you start more accursed than this loathsome profligacy? [Then follows Thyestes and his meals, &c., the Scythians, who eat lice, but are not cannibals, &c. Porphyry continues] What, then, does this saying mean? For even though it were meant to be taken in a mystical or allegorical sense, still the mere sound of the words grates inevitably on the soul and makes it rebel against a loathsome saying . . . unsuitable and alien to the habits of a noble life.

The Christian apologist might have pleaded that other religions had their mysteries and yet escaped persecution. Suspicion in the case of all mysteries was inevitable, in fact, one of the charms which made initiation so sought after by a blasé society. The worship of Cybele and Mithra, for instance, had its *taurobolium*. To the Fathers of the Church this seemed a travesty of the Cross; but in its origin it goes back to times before Calvary. The rite took place, as a rule, in early spring, and was often prolonged for two or three days. Only seventeen years before the massacre of the Christians at Lyons (177) there had been a great *taurobolium* at this capital of Gaul, the record of which is still preserved for us. The ceremony was superintended by the magistrates and attended by a vast crowd of people. With many solemn forms the consecrated bull was lifted on to a platform and slaughtered. Meanwhile the devotees were placed in a trench beneath, that they might bathe in the streams of blood and thus obtain strength and purification. The effect of this sacrament was supposed to last for twenty years without the need of renewal. The devotee who died in the interval could engrave on his tomb the record of his cleansing in the phrase, whose claims so stirred the wrath of the Christians, *renatus in æternum*, 'born again to eternal life'.

The *taurobolium* was a costly public function available only for the few. But there were other mysteries secret in their nature, attempts to lift the veil of Isis, to penetrate by strange symbols and rites into the inner secret of Pantheism. 'What I saw there,' writes one of these initiates, Apuleius, who for once ceases to be a mere sensualist—

I would tell if it were lawful . . . I trode the confines of death and the threshold of Proserpine. I was swept round all the elements and returned. I beheld the sun at midnight shining with purest radiance. Gods of heaven and gods of hell! I saw you face to face and adored in presence.

But Mithraism, the worship of Isis, and other religions had all taken steps, as we have seen, to avoid persecution. The mysteries of the Christians, on the other hand, were the secrets of men who would not stoop to secure either official sanction or popular support, but who yet, by the very necessities of their religion and its mission, were aggressive, perhaps at times imprudent, enthusiasts.

This imprudent aggression especially manifested itself in frequent 'atheistic' attacks upon heathen temples and ritual, in themselves sufficient explanation of the persecuting fury of the mob. 'If you will give me leave,' said Symphorian of Autun to the judge, 'I should like to smash this image of a devil with a mallet.' In spite of the official discouragement of the Church, the spirit of Symphorian animated the more stalwart of its adherents. A few illustrations will show how this issued in martyrdom. We may take the case of Leo of Patara, an aged ascetic of

Asia Minor, whose friend Paregorius had suffered death in the persecution of Decius.

Now it happened in those days that the proconsul Lollianus came to Patara and celebrated the feast of Serapis, taking occasion against the Christians and compelling all to sacrifice to idols. And when many were hastening to the temple Leo withdrew in indignation to the place where rested the bones of the blessed martyr Paregorius. There he poured out his wonted supplications and returned home, wrapped in the thought of the glorious deeds of his friend. After a while he fell asleep and dreamed a dream. He thought that he saw a mighty storm, and a raging torrent, with Paregorius and himself in the midst of the floods, for he found it not difficult to reach Paregorius. When he awoke he set out at once for the burial-place of his friend, nor would he choose a quiet road, but the one which lay through the midst of the market. And when he came to the temple (of Fortune) and saw the lanterns and tapers burning before the shrine, he tore down the lanterns with his hands, and trampled the tapers beneath his feet, crying out the while: 'If you think the gods have any power let them defend themselves.'

The inevitable result followed. On his return to the city – for the outrage would seem to have taken place very early in the morning – Leo was arrested. To the charges brought against him Leo's only answer was a somewhat irrelevant lecture to the judge on the doctrines of Christianity. Taking pity on his white hairs, Lollianus offered to forgo the act of sacrifice if only Leo would repeat after him the words, 'Great are the gods.' 'Yes,' replied the old man, 'great in destroying the souls of those who believe in them.' At length the patience of Lollianus gave way. He sentenced Leo to be dragged to the top of a high rock and pitched into the torrent which flowed through the town. 'But that brave athlete of Christ', worn out with the lashings, died on the way.

Even when innocent of actual outrage on the temples or rites the Christians at times acted almost as indiscreetly. We may instance Romanus, a deacon and exorcist of Antioch, who tried to stop a heathen procession. For this he was condemned by Galerius to lose his tongue (17 Nov. 303).

The case of Theodore the Tiro or recruit, sympathetically related for us by Gregory of Nyssa, was of a more daring order. Arrested for his Christianity, he was brought before the authorities of Amasea, the capital of Pontus. When asked why he would not sacrifice, the rough enthusiast replied—

I know nothing of your gods. They don't exist. You are wrong in calling seducing imposters of devils by the name of gods. My God is Christ, the only begotten Son of God.

An officer with a reputation for wit mockingly asked him: 'How is it,

Theodore, your God has a Son?' Theodore replied by a quotation from his Catechism, that would be perfectly unintelligible to the bystanders, then happily retorted upon his questioner by asking him about the favourite cult of Amasea, the worship of the Great Mother. The authorities, pleased with his readiness, gave him a little time for 'reconsidering his insanity'. Theodore used his reprieve for a different purpose. That night he set on fire the temple of the Great Mother. Building and statue were alike reduced to ashes. Theodore made no attempt to escape, but boldly proclaimed the deed. His defence before the magistrates was an impossible assertion of the individualistic standpoint. He was condemned to be burnt, and 'so passed to God by a splendid road', singing as he went: 'I will bless the Lord at all times; His praise shall continually be in my mouth.'

VI

The governing classes persecuted Christianity because they saw clearly its political danger; the lower classes had an intense hatred for the new religion, because it was a thing apart. The two causes were in reality one; ignorance and imperialism were united in their hatred of the individualistic spirit. 'The language of sedition,' said Celsus, 'is only used by those who separate and stand aloof from the society of their fellows.' The Christians were a peculiar people, with peculiar views of their own. Though, unlike the philosophers, they wore no distinctive garb – unless, indeed, absence of ostentation be counted a garb – in this world, they were yet not of the world. 'We are supposed,' writes Tertullian, 'to live aloof from crowds.' Their opponents, it is true, phrased the matter differently: 'a people who skulk and shun the light of day, silent in public, but garrulous in their holes and corners'; 'people who separate themselves and break away from the rest of mankind'. Their very titles among themselves were peculiar, a sign of this 'breaking away', a barbarous jargon of their own – 'little fish', 'the new-born', 'the newly caught', and the like. Nor could the conscientious Christian save himself from thrusting forward his peculiarities before a society which had surrounded every act of life with pagan ritual. For, as Milman has well put it:

Paganism met him in every form, in every quarter, in every act and function of every day's business; not merely in the graver offices of the State, but in the civil and military acts of public men; in the senate which commenced its deliberations with sacrifice; in the camp, the centre of which was a consecrated temple. The Pagan's domestic hearth was guarded by the Penates, or by the ancestral gods of his family or tribe; by land he travelled under the protection of one tutelar divinity, by sea of another; the birth, the bridal, the funeral had each its presiding deity; the very commonest household utensils were cast in mythological forms; he could scarcely drink without being reminded of libations to the gods; and the language itself was impregnated with constant allusions to the popular religion.

That the 'peculiarity' of Christianity exposed its disciples to various persecutions needs no evidence. The same has happened in every age and clime, is happening today on every mission-field. But when we pass from this general statement to particulars, when we try to estimate the precise measure of 'peculiarity', and the precise effect of the spirit of aloofness upon the daily life of the Church, we are met with difficulties. Writers of diverse schools have too often idealized the early Church, in forget-fulness of the exact parallel furnished by modern work among the heathen. Then, as now, many Christians brought with them into their new religion the habits and faults of their old life. Only the more stal-wart succeeded in disengaging themselves completely from their pagan environment. The ordinary converts did not, as a rule, alter the outward appearance of their lives; nor did they, for that matter, supply the martyrs with whose records we are dealing. But when we leave the unknown multitude of average and probably somewhat commonplace converts, and turn to the leaders and teachers of the Church, our per-plexities are by no means at an end. Even stalwarts must live, and to some extent conform to the usages of society. Where to draw the line was a matter of debate, upon which the Church was hopelessly divided. Then, as now, there were two parties; the one, which for lack of a better term we may call the Puritan, making up for the fewness of its numbers by dogmatism and devotion; the other, probably the more cultured, cer-tainly the more influential, but hampered by the lack of logic and utter-ance so generally characteristic of the *via media*. A few, if we may judge from their writings, tried to belong to both parties, and to prove that there was really no difference between the two views. Of these last the most eloquent and persuasive is the anonymous author of the well-known *Epistle to Diognetus*. The writer, in an oft-quoted passage, pleads that

Christians are not distinguished from the rest of mankind either in locality or in speech or in customs. For they dwell not somewhere in cities of their own, neither do they use some different language, nor practise an extra-ordinary (παράσημον) manner of life. But while they dwell in cities of Greeks and barbarians, as the lot of each is cast, and follow the native customs in dress, food, and the other arrangements of life, yet the constitution of their own citizenship which they set forth is marvellous, and confessedly contra-dicts expectation. They dwell in their own countries, but only as sojourners.

They bear their share in all things as citizens, and they endure all hardships as strangers. Every foreign country is a fatherland to them, and every fatherland is foreign.

This matter of the relation of the Christian to the current life of his age is of such importance, not merely for the study of martyrdom and renunciation in general, but for the gaining a correct insight into the inner life of the Church of the martyrs, that we propose to examine it more fully. For in it lay not the least of the causes of hatred and persecution.

We may dismiss at once the extremists of both types; those on the one hand whose laxity of conviction or conduct defended even attendance at the degrading public spectacles, quoting scripture to their purpose, and those who from extreme parousian standpoints made life of any sort practically impossible. The sincere Christian who tried to follow the light, and yet act out his part as citizen and neighbour found difficulties enough confront him, without inventing the impasses of a rigid logic.

Logic in fact, then as now, rarely formed the final arbiter by whose decision the affairs of life were settled. We have an interesting illustration of this in the names of the Christian. The martyrs perished because they declined to sacrifice to gods whose very names they bore – Apollos, Apollonius, Dionysius, Hermas, Saturninus, Phœbe, and the like. Not until the age of persecution had ceased do Christian names, i.e. names from the Old or New Testament, for instance Mary, begin to displace the old heathen names. Even then Christians were more frequently called by the name of some distinguished martyr, whose blood had washed it from its original heathen stain. In this matter 'the general custom of the world in which people were living proved stronger than any reflections of their own'. The early Christians, with rare common sense, declined to strain out the gnats while the real problems and difficulties still awaited solution. A public change of name would have been a dangerous advertisement of their new faith. But when prudence was no longer of any avail, the Christians in the fourth century often changed their pagan names for others more hallowed by association, before they met their death. 'One martyr,' writes Procopius of Gaza, 'called himself Jacob, another Israel, another Jeremiah, another Daniel, and having taken these names they readily went forth to martyrdom.'

The question of names was not of much importance. But the relation of the Christian to the business life of the world was no small difficulty. In an age when manual work was considered as suitable only for slaves, the Church insisted thereon as a duty; but some, for instance Tertullian, whose fervid nature admits nothing short of the ideal, can scarcely find an occupation in which the Christian could engage without compromise with idolatry. To those who pleaded that if they followed his advice they would be cut off from every means of livelihood, Tertullian answers that 'faith must despise starvation as much as it despises death.' His indignation with the Christian manufacturer of idols we can understand – 'how can a man raise in the worship of God hands that have made idols?' but he carries his logic to the prohibition of all trades engaged however indirectly in supplying the needs of idol-makers, e.g. goldbeaters and engravers.

'With what face,' he asks, 'can a Christian dealer in incense, who happens to pass a temple, spit on the smoking altars; and puff aside their fumes when he himself has sold the very material for the altar?' *Ib. de Idol.* 2.

That no Christian could be an actor or gladiator, or teach acting, is intelligible, but Tertullian would bar the Christian from becoming a schoolmaster, since it involved the teaching the names and myths of the gods. For 'that idolatry which is midwife to us all' still ruled the schools in the shape of Greek and Latin literature, and, in spite of the protests of Tertullian and Jerome and Gregory the Great, was destined still to rule them.

The question whether a Christian could become a teacher is so characteristic of the general difficulty that it deserves fuller examination. The emphatic negative of Tertullian and his school did not, we imagine, commend itself to many, though inscriptions, it is true, give us the names of but few Christian schoolmasters. Inasmuch as Tertullian did not counsel the withdrawal of Christian children from the schools – 'studying literature is allowable, but not teaching' – his advice would simply have led to the depriving the little ones of all teachers whose example and silent influence might have done something to counteract the secular and pagan education. The *Canons of Hippolytus*, of the same age probably as Tertullian, are more practical in allowing the convert to continue to act as school-master, on condition of reciting a sentence of his creed before the lessons, 'Non est deus nisi Pater et Filius et Spiritus Sanctus.' They urge, also, that the Christian teacher should use his influence, if possible, to win over some of his heathen pupils to the faith in Christ. No doubt the difficulties confronting a Christian grammarian were considerable. In a chapter of his *Confessions* Augustine declaims against

the hellish torrent of use and custom which sweeps away the sons of Eve into that vast and stormy sea which scarcely they who have embarked upon the tree (i.e. the cross) can pass in safety.

He is speaking of the school lessons, the shower of gold in the lap of

Danaë, and the like, 'the wine of error held to our lips by drunken teachers!' Nor were the heathen text-books and the constant declamations on mythological topics the sole trouble. Holidays and payment were alike associated with heathen rites and deities. The first fee was the due of Minerva; at the feast of Flora the schoolroom must be adorned with garlands. The necessary aloofness of the Christian teacher from most of his boys both in the social and religious life would not make matters easier. Of all this we have an illustration, extreme, perhaps, and yet to some extent characteristic, in the case of the martyred schoolmaster Cassian of Imola (*Forum Cornelii*). This man, who was, it must be confessed, somewhat of a martinet, as in fact were most schoolmasters in those days, was arrested in the midst of his work. On refusing to sacrifice, he was handed over to his lads. They bound his hands and stabbed him to death with their sharp pens (*acutis stylis*).

That the Church made no attempt to provide schools of its own for children will not excite surprise. This would have led to the very identification which the more part were anxious to avoid. The school system of the Empire was too well established and endowed for the attempt to succeed, unless supported by larger resources than the Church could command. But in the case of Christians thrown out of a situation by their conversion, especially actors and others similarly engaged, the Church sought to ease the strain by itself providing work for its members. We see this clearly brought out in a passage of the *Didaché*, where it forms part of a section on the duties of the Church to the brethren on their journeys:

But let every one that cometh in the name of the Lord be received. If the comer is a traveller, assist him, so far as ye are able, but he shall not stay with you more than two or three days, if it be necessary. But if he wishes to settle with you, being a craftsman, let him work for and eat his bread. But if he has no craft, according to your wisdom provide how he shall live as a Christian among you, but not in idleness. If he will not do this, he is trafficking upon Christ.

In the *Apostolic Constitutions* this becomes one of the manifold charitable duties so characteristic of the early Church, the discharge of which fell upon the bishop:

Exhibit to the orphan the care of parents; to the widows the care of husband; to those of suitable age marriage; for the artificer obtain work; to the incapable give alms; for strangers provide an home; for the sick visitation; for prisoners assistance; . . . for the young orphan help that he may learn a trade.

Naturally, with the growth of the Church such methods became unworkable, in part because of the 'trafficking upon Christ' of rogues, of whom Peregrinus may be taken as a sample, who found that to pass as a Christian by means of the secret signs, the fish and the like, enabled them to live in luxury at the expense of the brethren. The existence of such a system of support proves the presence in the Church from its earliest days of a fair proportion of wealthy men, without whose generous gifts such a scheme could not have been attempted.

The effect of all this on the aloofness of the Christian, and the consequent gulf between himself and other classes, will not need illustration. The system worked in two ways. Early Christianity was essentially a brotherhood founded upon a gospel of love and charity. As such it stood apart from its surroundings. At the same time, by its exaltation of the value and need of work, there can be little doubt, though the matter is not capable, perhaps, of formal proof, that this brotherhood, in spite of the fact that they were necessarily shut out from certain trades, won for itself no small wealth. In a population bent on 'bread and the games', which had long handed over to slaves the pursuit of industry, where a middle class scarcely existed, an earnest, industrious brotherhood, which shunned as 'works of the devil' the amusements and idleness which sapped the life of the Roman world, could not fail to prosper. But the more they prospered, the more they would draw down upon themselves the hatred of their neighbours, who, from causes into which we cannot now enter, but which finally dragged down in financial ruin the Roman Empire itself, were daily growing poorer.

From the difficulties of business we pass to the questions of social intercourse and daily life. The consistent Christian – inconsistent Christians, alas! abounded – was never seen at theatre, circus, or Coliseum. 'Where more,' said Tertullian, bluntly, 'will you find the devil with his angels?' But outside these acknowledged restrictions there was then, as now, a large and often doubtful borderland of duty. On Caesar's birthday should the Christian illuminate his house, and festoon his gates with wreaths? Could the Christian attend the weddings, funerals, birthday rejoicings, and other festivities in the homes of heathen friends? Could matters be conveniently arranged by leaving out on the invitation card the words 'to assist at a sacrifice'? If the Christian was sick, should he seek shelter in the hospitals attached to the temples of Aesculapius, in whose long dormitories, when the lamps were lighted, the priests of the god of healing recited the vesper prayers? If he were wronged, must he refuse to appear in the law-courts, the business and forms of which were mixed up with heathen rites?

From many offices in the State, the duties of which involved the performance of heathen rites, the conscientious Christian, in the opinion of many, was necessarily excluded. For office involved not only pagan sacrifice, but 'the holding spectacles either at his own or the State's expense', 'the presiding at the same', to say nothing of judicial duties which could not be carried out 'without chaining and torturing'. 'The Christian,' said Tertullian, 'has no desire to be aedile'; he classes 'politics' (*res publicae*) among the things that are 'alien', for 'the Christian has but one commonwealth – the world', a doctrine which drew forth the taunt of Celsus: 'Were all to behave as you do, the affairs of this world would fall into the hands of wild and lawless barbarians.' Tertullian does not mention that the expenses of office in the second century (much more so in the third) had become so great as to involve financial ruin for all but the wealthiest. Others besides Christians caught at every means of escape from the intolerable burden. Some went so far as to unfit themselves by marriage with a slave; others bought themselves out at a price. The Christian's excuse of religion would seem to his neighbour either cant or selfishness, if not the cloak of a heavy bribe, unless accompanied, as in the case of Cyprian and Basil, by such a surrender of their property as would put them outside the list of those eligible for office. There are grounds also for believing that Christians, for whom escape from office proved impossible, tried to shelter themselves by a policy which outsiders rightly or wrongly dubbed as 'laziness'. We can well imagine that they would do no more in the matter of spectacles than they were obliged. Some, it is true, tried to perform to the full all their municipal functions, including the bowing in the house of Rimmon, and excused themselves by the examples of Joseph and Danial, who, 'clean from idolatry', wore 'the livery and purple of the prefecture'. That there was no direct command of the Church in the age of Tertullian against taking office is shown by the *Canons of Hippolytus*, as well as by the later decision of the Council of Elvira, and the number of Christians who actually took office. But it was acknowledged that office should only be undertaken as the last resort, while escape from it can scarcely be classed as renunciation.

Finally there was the question of the army, the symbol of patriotism, the refuge of a trembling world against the barbarians. Should the Christian serve at all, or, if unable to escape this obligation, what was his duty? Opinion on the army varied considerably. Tertullian held that 'there could be no agreement between the human and divine *sacramentum*, the standard of Christ and the devil, the camp of light and the camp of darkness,' and went so far as to urge desertion. He was followed by Lactantius and Origen. When Celsus pointed out the consequences, Origen fell back at first on Providence – in reality he becomes a fatalist – and then ended the argument by stating that all Christians are priests, and as priests are exempt from military service, but will 'form an army of piety, and fight by offering prayers'. He definitely states that 'Christians will not fight, even if the king (emperor) requires us to do'. Similar decisions might be quoted from others of the Fathers.

The difficulty of a Christian becoming or continuing as a soldier was not merely theological, but practical. A Christian in the army, if appointed a non-commissioned officer, for instance a centurion, was bound to perform, or at least to witness in silence, certain sacrifices or else resign at once office and life. This happened in many cases, of some of which we still possess the records. We may take as an example the story of Marcellus, 'a centurion of the Trajan legion' stationed at Tangiers. The birthday of Maximian was being celebrated with the usual sacrifices (21 July), when Marcellus, horrified with all that he saw around him, suddenly flung away his military belt and his centurion's vine-stick and cried,

I am a soldier of Jesus Christ, the eternal King. I have done with fighting for your emperors. I despise the worship of deaf and dumb gods of wood and stone. If the terms of service are such that one is bound to offer sacrifices to gods and emperors, then I refuse to be a soldier.

He was, of course, arrested and tried (30 Oct).

'How come you to be so mad as to renounce your oath and speak like that?' asked the deputy prefect. 'There is no madness in those who serve the Lord,' was the reply. 'Did you say the very words given here in the commandant's report?' 'I did.' 'Did you throw away your vine-stick?' 'I did.'

As he was led away to be beheaded, Marcellus turned to the prefect; 'God bless you,' he said. 'That,' adds the writer of this old record, 'was the proper way in which a martyr should take leave of the world.'

The difficulty of sacrifices scarcely applied to the rank and file. But there were other dangers that the Christian soldier ran, an illustration of which will be found in the recently published story of Dasius, of the army of Moesia. The troops there were accustomed to elect one of their number to act as 'king' during the Saturnalia, the annual heathen feast of slaves, now supplanted by Christmas. After thirty days of rule this 'king' was expected to offer himself as a sacrifice to Saturn. When the lot fell upon Dasius he refused to act, pleading that he was a Christian. Needless to say, he suffered the consequences.

Moreover, the army, at the time when Tertullian and Origen wrote, was carried away by the cult of Mithraism. Throughout Europe, as Cumont has shown, the 'Invincible Saviour' Mithra was at this time the special deity of solders. Dacia and Pannonia, for instance, the great military outposts of the Empire, are full of his shrines; the spread of Mithraism in Pannonia, especially in the chain of Roman defences along the

Danube, being the work of the auxiliaries of two legions, the second and fifteenth, whose recruiting ground was Cappadocia. In one camp no less than three Mithraeums have been discovered. From the Danube the religion was carried to the two Germanies, probably by the eighth legion, in or about the year A.D. 20. Along the Rhine from Basel to Cologne, and especially in the military district between the Main and the Neckar, the temples and inscriptions of Mithra are to be seen everywhere. From this stronghold of the faith the triumphant march of Mithra may be traced by Cologne, Treves, and Boulogne, the station of the British fleet, to the great port of London and the camps of Caerleon, Chester, and York; while five guard-houses in the wall of Hadrian, as well as an outpost among the Cheviots, still show the shrines of the god. All this added complication to a situation difficult enough already. To enter the army, or to remain in it after conversion, involved a Christian profession in the midst of a specially organized and aggressive heathenism.

There was also a theological or theoretical difficulty of some importance. The Christians, influenced by the words of Jesus and of St. Paul, had from the first adopted the conception of the Church as the *Militia Christi*, the army of Christ. They were 'soldiers' in a 'holy war' which should bring in 'with violence' the kingdom of heaven. Jesus was their *Imperator*, that great Captain, to whom they were bound in allegiance by no common *sacramentum*, or oath; under whose standard, the Cross – the *vexillum Christi* – they were enrolled, and whose last words had been an earnest of victory: 'Be of good cheer: I have conquered the world.' But how can a man serve two Emperors, be enrolled under two flags, live in two camps, or go on two different campaigns at the same time? Does not the one exclude the other? So powerful indeed in the Early Church was this military metaphor, that many acted or rather reasoned as if it were a reality. They were 'the army of the living God', prepared, if need be, to become 'the army of martyrs' rather than deny their Captain. One of these stalwarts, a youth called Maximilian of Theveste, was pressed as a recruit, and on his refusal to serve was brought before the proconsul Dion. The magistrate ordered the attendants to measure him. 'He is five foot ten,' was the answer. 'Enroll him then at once,' said Dion. 'Cut off my head if you like,' cried the youth, 'but I cannot be a soldier of the world, I am a soldier of my God.' They hung the leaden badge of service round his neck. 'I don't accept it,' he said; 'I have already the badge of service under Christ.' So he persisted to the end, and with 'a bright smile' obtained his 'crown.' 'Give to the executioner,' he said, turning to his father, 'the soldier's dress you made ready for me.'

Such cases as that of Maximilian were rare; not many soldiers were impressed against their will. In spite of all difficulties, theological or practical, the Christians in the army were fairly numerous. The story of the 'Thundering Legion', whatever be its value otherwise, proves conclusively that the views of Origen and Tertullian were not accepted by the early Church, which preferred to point to the many Christian soldiers in the pages of the New Testament, above all to the story of the believing centurion at the foot of the cross.

Then, as now, there were soldiers not a few who could be as patriotic as Celsus himself, and as firm for their faith, when occasion called, as Tertullian. The army never lacked Christians, true heroes of God, who were prepared, if need be, to lay down their lives rather than deny their Christ. The proportion of martyr-soldiers is uncommonly large, and is, no doubt, to be explained by the fact that in times of stress and persecution the detection of Christians who were soldiers was easy, escape, in other words desertion, impossible; while the first effort of the Government when persecution broke out would be directed to the purging the army of the accursed taint. The number of Christians who refused to serve and suffered in consequence would appear to have been but few; the Christians in the army who laid down their lives for their Lord and Master form a goodly company. These were they of whom the seer had his vision, 'the armies in heaven which follow the Word upon white horses, clothed in fine linen, white and clean'. (Rev. 19: 14.)

Such were some of the difficulties with which the Christian was daily faced. The answer he gave varied. Some, as we have seen, led on by Tertullian, took up a position of irreconcilable aloofness from life, which led Celsus and others to urge that Christianity constituted a danger to the social fabric itself. Others found that in practice, provided only that they maintained a certain reserve, difficulties were less real than they appeared. For them *solvitur ambulando* proved a better guide than logic. They did their best in that state of life in which God had placed them, to keep themselves unspotted from the world. These, as Tertullian owns in an oft-quoted passage wrung from him by the needs of his *Apology*, formed the vast majority of the Church. Christians, he claims, are not *infructuosi in negotiis*, 'of no use in the affairs of life'.

'How can that be when we dwell beside you, sharing your mode of life, dress, habits? We are not Brahmins or Indian gymnosophists dwelling in woods and exiled from life. We live beside you in the world, making use of the same forum, market, bath, shop, inn, and all other places of trade. We sail with you, fight shoulder to shoulder, till the soil, and traffic with you.'

Christians, in fact, in the third century were to be met with everywhere, in business, in all positions of the State, in the army, and even in the

Senate. But their presence in these positions was surrounded with many difficulties; they could scarcely avoid arousing popular suspicion both by what they did and by what they left undone. With the best will in the world, they remained a peculiar people, who must be prepared at any moment to meet the storm of hatred.

The hatred was the more acute because the Christians were not only peculiar, but proud of their peculiarities, by which, as they claimed, they rose superior to the world. To Celsus they seemed, in their admixture of humility and pride,

frogs in council on a marsh, worms in synod on a dunghill, quarrelling as to which is the greatest sinner, and yet declaring that God announces all things to us beforehand. . . . Land and water, air and stars, all things are for our sake and are appointed to serve us.

The Christians, in their own proud phrase, were 'the new people', 'the third race' – this last, possibly, of Gentile rather than Christian origin, though adopted by them without demur. Such titles were not merely the signs of separation and aloofness; they were the assertions of a purpose. The Christians claimed that they would accomplish a task which in the end baffled the Empire – build into a new unity the diverse nations of earth.

VII

The most powerful cause of hatred yet remains. The Christians professed that 'nothing was more alien to them than politics'; in reality, from the standpoint of the Roman governor, they were intense politicians of a most dangerous type. The Christians were condemned, not because of their theological views, but because of their supreme loyalty to a law and throne outside the Roman law and throne. They were not anxious to run counter to the law and customs of the Empire; they were, in fact, unanimous in upholding them. But if at any time such law and customs came into conflict with the will of God, as interpreted by themselves and their standards, they must obey God rather than man. To the Roman executive, which demanded absolute submission of will and life from all its subjects, such a doctrine could not be other than a danger to the State, once its purport was clear. They could not overlook the existence in their midst of 'a new people', 'a third race', of cosmopolitan character, who proclaimed openly that 'they looked for a kingdom'; who went so far as to 'frame laws for themselves according to their own purposes, and observed these laws', and refused to obey any laws which ran contrary thereto, and who daily grew in numbers, influence, and wealth.

Nothing is more natural than the political disgust and hatred which the Christians in consequence aroused. If today powerful governments take alarm lest the fealty of Roman Catholics to the Pope should prove stronger under certain circumstances than their allegiance to the state, if the doctrine of Passive Resistance excites suspicion among many who claim that a man cannot be a loyal citizen who accepts its basis, we can well imagine the hatred that would well out against the Christians when first they asserted these startling doctrines in a world whose fabric, civil and religious, was built upon the absolutism of Caesar. Even the great political maxim of Jesus, 'Render unto Caesar the things that are Caesar's, and unto God the things that are God's,' becomes meaningless, if not treasonable, in a state that made little difference between Caesar and God.

The refusal, moreover, of the Christians to worship Caesar was naturally interpreted by judge and mob as a confession of disloyalty to the Empire and its head. In not a few of their trials, which for the most part resolve themselves into cases of high treason, we find the Christians protesting their loyalty and devotion to Caesar, but at the same time laying emphasis upon its limits. Said one of the Scillitan martyrs, 'We give honour to Caesar as Caesar; we offer worship (*timorem*) to God alone.' This was, in fact, in their case, as in that of the majority of Christians, the cause of their condemnation. We see this clearly brought out in their formal sentence:

Speratus and the rest having confessed that they are Christians, and having refused to render worship to Caesar, I pronounce that they be punished with the sword.

Tertullian is equally explicit:

Therefore as to what relates to the honour due to kings or emperors, we have sufficiently laid it down that it behoves us to render all obedience, according to the apostle's precept, but within the limits of our discipline and provided that we keep ourselves free from idolatry (*De Idol.* 15).

The popular feeling in this matter was correct. Many passages no doubt can be adduced expressive of the utmost loyalty. A beautiful Litany for those

to whom Thou hast given the power of sovereignty, through Thine excellent and unspeakable might, that we, knowing the glory and honour which Thou hast given them, may submit ourselves unto them; . . . Grant unto them, therefore, O Lord, that they may administer the government which Thou hast given them without failure.

forms the conclusion of the letter of the first apostolic Father, who in this was but following the example of St. Paul. Prayers for the emperors, in fact, constituted a fixed part of the organization of Christian worship from the first. Tertullian gives us a moving picture of the Church on its knees for Caesar, 'with hands outspread, with head uncovered, without a prompter', and with bitter irony exhorts the magistrates 'to draw forth with tortures the souls that are thus loyally pleading with God' for one whom the Christians hold to be 'second to God alone'. 'The Christian,' he argues,

is the enemy of no man, assuredly not of the Emperor, whom he knows to be ordained of God. Of necessity therefore he loves, reveres, and honours him, and prays for his safety, with that of the whole Roman Empire, that it may endure – as endure it will – as long as the world itself (*ad Scap.* 2).

But Tertullian was writing an apology. In our judgement the Apocalypse, or the Christian interpellations in the *Sibylline Oracles*, represents much more accurately the real view of the early Church upon the Empire. The noble conception which St. Paul had formed of using the Empire and its institutions as a means for the spread of Christianity was one natural to a Roman citizen; in practice Christianity and the Empire proved fundamentally antagonistic, if only because they were rivals in conception and method. Each claimed to be a kingdom of universal sway; each created a Church of universal obligation, each demanded absolute fealty to its supreme Lord. Between Caesar and Christ there could be no compromise, at any rate on the existing footing of Caesar. When Celsus pleaded that the ideas of Christians, if carried out, meant the destruction of existing society, he was but urging a truth hidden from Origen and other apologists.

Such were, in the main, the causes of the charge against Christianity of 'hostility to the race or state'. From the standpoint of our present purpose the reader should note that persecution was the direct outcome of the Christian doctrine of renunciation. For the causes which led to popular and official hatred were not theological, or the outcome of esoteric doctrines of worship, or the result of certain ethical postulates. Nor were they the result of religious animosity. Polytheism as such is indifferent whether a man worship one God or twenty. They were rather the outcome of the fundamental tenet of primitive Christianity, that the Christian ceased to be his own master, ceased to have his old environment, ceased to hold his old connexions with the state; in everything he became the bond-servant of Jesus Christ, in everything owing supreme allegiance and fealty to the new Empire and the Crucified Head. 'We engage in these conflicts,' said Tertullian, 'as men whose very lives are not our own ... We have no master but God.' 'What is thy condition?'

said the judge to the martyr Maximus. 'I am a free man,' was the reply, 'but the slave of Christ.' Similar was the answer of Febronia, a wealthy and beautiful virgin. 'A slave!' asked the judge Selenus, in surprise; 'whose slave?' 'The slave of Christ.' But the rise of the 'slaves of Christ' meant the fall of the rule of the Caesars. As St. John saw clearly, the Empire ($K\acute{o}\sigma\mu os$) was bound to hate the Church. Nor was the hatred the less because the Empire knew that it was in the pangs of dissolution; 'the world,' said the seer, 'is passing away.'

Chapter Four

THE GREAT PERSECUTIONS

I

THE reader who has followed our investigation will be in a position to answer the further question: Were the martyrs of the Early Church many or few? The question is not one of mere statistics or curiosity. Especially is the answer of importance for our present purpose. Was this supreme renunciation a rare or common event, a factor so infrequent that so far as the general run of Christians is considered it might be neglected; or was persecution, or at any rate the fear of it, part of the price that each Christian was called upon to pay? Unfortunately, the question, at the best not easy to answer, has become mixed up with theological polemics. Some have represented the Roman magistrates as men of singular humanity and moderation, whose 'philosophy' led them, as a rule, to decline the task of persecution, or who, at most, singled out here and there some Christian distinguished in rank or influence by whose death they might strike terror into the whole sect. Others, on the other hand, have reckoned the battalions of the 'noble army of martyrs' as almost inexhaustible. 'There is no day in the whole year,' wrote Jerome, in his epistle to Heliodorus, 'unto which the number of five thousand martyrs cannot be ascribed, except only the first day of January.' But compared with later stories the computation of Jerome was moderate. It is, at any rate, somewhat borne out by the statement of Eusebius, that in the persecution in the Thebias as many as one hundred martyrs a day were often sacrificed, 'so that the weapons of the murderers were completely blunted'.

The truth, as is generally the case, lies between the two extremes. We may dismiss at once the incredible legends, in which the mediaeval Church delighted, of the thousands of virgins or soldiers slain at Cologne, on Mount Ararat, and the like. Accuracy in figures is but a modern foible. But with equal justice may we claim as an exaggeration the idea that the penal laws against the Christians were not put into force, save at certain rare and infrequent intervals. The Christians, like the anarchists of Russia, were always liable to persecution and death; the smouldering fires of popular hatred or official zeal might break out against them at any moment. They lived from day to day conscious of a danger to which they were exposed, and which some act of indiscretion on their part might bring to a head. We may grant that the outbreak of persecution in systematic form was an infrequent occurrence; depending chiefly on local circumstances of popular feeling, on the zeal, superstition, or humanity of the district magistrates. There were, however, seasons of special activity in persecution – enumerated by the early Church as ten in all – when the hatred against the Christians burst forth, not locally, but over wide areas. The history of these great persecutions, their causes, special features, and results, claims our notice.

Hitherto in our treatment, in order that we might the better grasp the broad outlines, we have neglected to some extent the notes of time. We have treated the age of persecution as if it were a unity in itself. Such a broad generalization of a movement stretching over a period of two hundred and fifty years, though advantageous for the simplification of our argument, needs of course considerable revision. There are, in fact, two main periods into which the history of persecution in the early Church may be divided. The one period, marked by outbreaks neither systematic nor severe, closes with the early years of the third century. The other period is characterized by a desperate struggle, or rather series of struggles, between the Empire and the Church, and closes with the triumph of the Church under Constantine. These two periods are not mere artificial marks of time. They correspond to a real distinction upon which too much stress cannot be laid. In the first period the Church was comparatively small and weak and by no means widely represented; in the second period the Empire woke up to discover a vast hostile organization created in its midst, whose rapid growth in every land was sweeping all before it. Thus in the first period persecution was fitful and local, the result rather of passing hates than clear statesmanship; in the second period the State bent all its energies to the task, deliberately undertaken, of crushing out the Church before it was too late. In the first period the number of martyrs was but few, for the Christians themselves were not numerous; in the second period there were times of wholesale massacre, though usually, as in other similar cases, the persecution was intensive rather than extensive.

II

The first of the ten persecutions, to follow for the time the traditional reckoning, was that of Nero. This, though certainly local rather than universal, stamped itself for ever upon the memory of the Church by reason of its fiendish cruelties as well as its distinguished victims. The number who suffered is unknown. Tacitus, it is true, speaks of a 'vast multitude' in Rome alone; but we have no means of checking his rhetoric. The total loss of the early written records of the Roman Church has robbed us of all names. Only with difficulty can we recover the story of St. Peter and St. Paul. The rest is a blank.

Under the Flavians there was a respite, so far, at any rate, as an organized persecution was concerned, until the second great outbreak under Domitian. The Christians were not alone in suffering from the cruel and suspicious nature of this tyrant. The inner secret of that sombre reign is still a mystery, but of the agony of the Roman world under his rule there can be no doubt. Domitian united ability and astuteness with timidity and cruelty. He seems to have been anxious, also, to conceal his vices, perhaps from himself, certainly from others, by a scrupulous devotion to the old forms of religion. So he flung his whole strength into a moral and religious reaction, and, in accordance with this design, sought to crush out the Christians. Domitian struck at the highest, putting to death 'as an innovator' ('quasi molitores rerum novarum') the ex-consul Acilius Glabrio, whom he had compelled (A.D. 91) to fight against a lion and two bears; also 'for atheism', Flavius Clemens, his cousin, who was either consul at that time or had but recently resigned the office, and whose two sons were Domitian's destined heirs in the Empire. On the same charge of 'atheism' he banished Clemens' wife Domitilla, his own niece, to Pontia, a little island in the Tyrrhene sea (A.D. 95). There in a narrow cell, in later years (385) visited by the lady Paula when on her travels, 'Domitilla drew out a long martyrdom for the confession of the Christian name.' Not long afterwards Domitian was slain by Stephen, the steward of Domitilla.

According to tradition, the wrath of Domitian fell on others in the Church even more illustrious than his cousins. He is said to have put to death Clement the Christian doctor, the third or fourth bishop of Rome. Tradition affirms that he struck at the aged apostle John. The apostle of love escaped, but how great was the danger of the Christians under this tyrant may be seen in the well-known tale, recorded by Dion, of Domitian's funeral banquet to a select number of nobles:

So he fitted up an apartment all in black. The ceiling was black, the walls were black, the pavement was black, and upon it were ranged rows of bare stone seats, black also. The guests were introduced at night without their attendants, and each might see at the head of his couch a column placed, like a tombstone, on which his own name was engraved, with a cresset lamp above it, such as is suspended in the tombs. Presently there entered a troop of naked boys, black also, who danced a horrid dance, and then stood still, offering the guests the morsels of food which are commonly presented to the dead. The guests were paralysed with terror, expecting death at every moment – the more so as, amid the deep silence of the company, Domitian spake of the things that appertain to the state of the dead (*Dio Cass*. lxvii 4).

In this case Domitian's delight in exquisite torture did not end tragically; but the result was generally otherwise. If Juvenal's satire is true, that even to talk with Domitian about the weather was to cast hazards for your life, how real was the peril of those who through allegiance to Christ disdained to ascribe to a suspicious madman the divinity on which he laid such stress! This tale points, moreover, to one characteristic of Domitian's persecution, as distinct from that of Nero. The Neronian persecution had proved 'a wholesale onslaught of reckless fury', somewhat restricted, it is true, in its area; that of Domitian was 'a succession of sharp, sudden, partial assaults, striking down one here and one there from malice or jealousy or caprice, and harassing the Church with an agony of suspense.'

III

The murder of Domitian ushered in the golden age of the Empire. From Nerva to Marcus Aurelius a succession of rulers of rare gifts and insight preserved the peace and prosperity of the world, in spite of the signs of growing bankruptcy and dissolution. But for the Church their rule was by no means a golden age of toleration. The depravity of a Nero or Domitian has too often led apologists and historians astray. As a matter of fact, it was not the worst emperors – a favourite fiction of the apologists in their appeal to the outside public – but the best who were the persecutors of the Church. The greater the vigilance of the emperor, the more determined he was to crush out sedition and disorder, the deeper his sense of responsibility for the preservation of the unity of his vast dominions, the more was he likely to come into conflict with so divisive a factor as the religion of Jesus. A great administrator, Trajan for instance, just because he was firm and vigilant, 'would send a Christian to punishment with no more hesitation and remorse than if it had been a question of a refractory soldier or a fugitive slave'.

The two great provincial emperors, Trajan and Hadrian, made no change of moment in the policy of their predecessors. The Roman view of Christianity is nowhere better illustrated than in the correspondence of Pliny and Trajan. In September, 111, Pliny the younger, a cultivated Roman lawyer, was sent out to restore order in the disorganized province of Bithynia-Pontus. About a year after his arrival, when sojourning, probably, at Amisus, in the eastern district of his rule, he received anonymous accusations charging 'many persons' with Christianity. The new religion, it seems, had taken considerable hold of the whole district, both in town and country. According to Pliny, who possibly exaggerated matters in order to magnify his vigilance, the temples were abandoned, the trade in sacrificial animals and in the fodder needful for their keep was in a parlous state. Acting on information volunteered, probably, by the aggrieved tradesmen, the police arrested the Christians, and Pliny examined them. The upshot was various. Some acknowledged the charge, and on the third time of asking were at once ordered off to execution as if they were assassins or coiners, while the Roman citizens among them were despatched to Rome to await Trajan's pleasure. There was no delay, no searching for precedents, no uncertain legal points on which advice might be necessary. The mere profession of Christianity was evidently a capital offence in itself, without the rest of refusal to worship the emperor. Some, however, denied, and substantiated their denial by offering wine and incense to Trajan as the fortune or guardian spirit of the Empire. Others claimed they had ceased to be Christians, in some cases, as far back as twenty-five years previous to the trial. Such were now willing to worship the emperor and curse Christ; to this last, owns Pliny, 'real Christians could never be forced.' Nevertheless they maintained that when they were Christians they had done nothing wrong:

'they had been accustomed to meet before daybreak on a fixed day that they might sing a hymn to Christ as God, to bind themselves by a mystic ordinance to commit no crime, neither be guilty of theft, robbery, adultery, the breaking of a promise, or the keeping back of a pledge.'

Later in the day they assembled, they said, for a common meal, probably the agapé, an action, they owned, contrary to the imperial edict against social clubs which Pliny had published immediately on his arrival.

To test this report Pliny examined by torture two slave women (*ancillae*), who were called deaconesses, but could discover nothing 'save a degrading and irrational superstition'. Pliny professed to feel in a dilemma. He apologizes that he had been without any previous experience of these investigations into the case of Christians, though the whole tone of his letter and his earlier persecution at Amisus show plainly that he is aware of a recognized method of law for dealing with crimes of this order. But his kindly nature prompts him to point out to Trajan certain difficulties, possibly in the hope of obtaining some mitigation of current procedure. Is he, he asks, to take into account extenuating circumstances such as youth? Is he to punish Christians simply because of their religion – for the Name, *nomen ipsum* – and therefore criminals *ipso facto*, or is he to decide by proved misdeeds? Further, should the accused recant, is that sufficient, without punishment for holding such baleful errors in the past?

Trajan answered that 'there can be no hard and fast rule.' Christians openly accused and convicted must be punished; that they purge themselves by performing heathen rites will suffice. Moreover, a magistrate may make this distinction between a thief or murderer and a Christian; he need not spend his time in hunting down the Christians until they were formally accused. Anonymous accusations, whether of Christianity or other crime, must be thrown into the paper basket; 'they form a bad precedent contrary to the real spirit of the age'.

Trajan's reply puts the matter into a nutshell. Tertullian, it is true, calls it a self-contradiction, and points out its mixture of Jedburgh justice and official laxity. But Tertullian was one of the hunted, and the logic of the persecuted and the persecutor are never in agreement. To us the decision seems clear. To be a Christian is to be an outlaw, as in fact Pliny had owned by his action at Amisus. But zeal should be tempered with discretion. So long as the Christians are kept in check, the magistrate need not hunt them down until he is obliged. The last is a detail of administration the wisdom or occasion of which each governor must decide for himself, for Trajan expressly refuses 'to lay down a general principle which may serve as a fixed rule of procedure'. The correspondence gives no indication that Trajan was inaugurating a new policy, commencing, as some have claimed, the systematic persecution of the Christians. Its whole drift, in fact, is rather the opposite – a desire on the part of Pliny to change a policy which he had discovered led to much suffering inflicted on harmless if deluded fanatics. Trajan's concessions also, such as they were, were changes in procedure rather than in the law. No clearer commentary upon the renunciation involved a century later in becoming a Christian can be found than the fact that the Christian apologists looked back to the days of Trajan as times of exceptional liberty. Two points in Trajan's letter told in their favour. The emperor plainly intimates that the magistrates must lead, not be led by popular hatred or private spleen. The necessity, again, of the presence of a formal accuser gave the Christians a general protection which, under various pleas, enabled merciful judges to dismiss a case when brought into court. Thus Tertullian tells us of a magistrate called Pudens, who, when a Christian was brought before him 'without the presence of the informer', tore the charge-sheet in pieces 'as not being consistent with the imperial edict'.

Trajan's successor, the Emperor Hadrian, another Spaniard of inferior character though almost equal administrative ability, appears to have made some slight alteration, more favourable to the Christians, in the legal procedure. The circumstances which gave rise to this rescript of Hadrian are, however, involved and difficult, though of the genuineness of the rescript itself there can be no reasonable doubt. The following seem to be the facts. Both in Greece and Asia the protection given to the Christians by Trajan against anonymous accusations had not proved sufficient. Informers and false witnesses abounded, and introduced by their methods a reign of terror. 'Delation' – the word is difficult to translate into the language of more favoured times, though probably there is a perfect equivalent in the Russian tongue – was one of the curses of the Empire, a recognized system even under the most blameless emperors. To turn informer was to enter a regular and lucrative profession. The legal fee for a successful delation was one-fourth of the estate of the condemned man. 'In no other way could a man so easily make himself a millionaire.' The Christians had no friends, and for some time the *delatores*, or false witnesses, reaped a golden reward. Thus far, as Hadrian's rescript shows, we are on certain ground. We may surmise that the existence of this reign of terror was brought to the notice of Hadrian by the Christians themselves. On the occasion of the emperor's second visit to his favourite Athens, in the winter of 128–9, a certain Christian, Quadratus by name – Eusebius states that he was also assisted by a converted philosopher called Marcianus Aristides – made some effort to appeal to him, and published the earliest Christian Apology of which we have record. According to a late and more than doubtful story, Hadrian had been willing to welcome Christ among his gods, and had ordered the building of temples that should be free from images, and so adapted for the new religion. We are told that he was only dissuaded by the report 'that all would become Christians if this were done, and the temples would be deserted'. Hadrian was known to be 'an eager explorer into all curiosities', who had sought initiation into the deepest mysteries of the heathen world. His insatiable curiosity – 'garrulous chattering', Julian called it – had an endless variety of moods, and at different times came under the influence of diverse creeds. But in one thing he was changeless – his sarcastic scepticism whether any creed was either genuine or worth belief. 'In Egypt,' he sneered—

'the Christians and the worshippers of Serapis are the same; those devoted to Serapis call themselves bishops of Christ. Rulers of synagogues, Samaritans. Christian presbyters are all astrologers, soothsayers, quacks; Christians, Jews, and Gentiles all alike worship money.'

In approaching such a cynic, Quadratus and his fellow-Christians would not be without hopes of success when they asked that the crime of Christianity should be brought under the regular law.

The efforts of Quadratus were of no avail. A rescript from Hadrian to Minicius (Minucius) Fundanus, the proconsul of Asia, gives the decision of the emperor. This important document ran as follows:—

I have received the letter sent me by your distinguished predecessor, Serenus Granianus, and am unwilling to pass over his report without reply, lest innocent persons be subjected to attack, and opportunity given to false accusers to despise them. If, therefore, it is manifest that the people of your province are wishful to support their complaints against the Christians by presenting formal charges against them on some point before your judgement-seat, I do not forbid them this course, though I will not allow them to resort to mere appeals and outcries. The fairer course, if any one wishes to bring an indictment, is, that you give a formal hearing. If, therefore, any one brings an indictment, and proves that the said Christians are committing any violation of the law, you are to punish them in proportion to their offences. But you must also take special care, if any one knowingly brings false charges against any man, that he be punished more severely because of this crime.

The meaning of the rescript is plain. To be a Christian was still in itself a crime, though the question of what constituted a Christian seems to have been left somewhat vague – no longer necessarily the name itself. The magistrate should see to it that he is not governed by the mob. The cry, 'Christians to the lions', must not take the place of a judicial investigation, and thereby cause the punishment of innocent men. The prosecutor, or *delator*, who failed to make good his case must be punished for false witness – a gain this of considerable value. Yet Hadrian, in spite of his liberalism, not to say licence of thought – 'half sceptic, half devotee, a scoffer and a mystic by turns', whose only settled conviction was probably the conviction that nothing can be settled—was driven into the formal allowance of the existing laws against Christianity. The lot of the Christians was still, as in the past, one of great uncertainty, at the best an unauthorized toleration liable at any moment, under the pressure of popular feeling, to give place to violent persecution. Though the records of but few cases of martyrdom under Hadrian have been preserved, nevertheless the Christian writers of that time, as we see from the *Shepherd* of Hermas, were ever haunted by the dread spectre of persecution.

IV

The two great emperors, Antoninus Pius and Marcus Antoninus (Aurelius) must also be numbered among the persecutors of the Church, the former, probably, in spite of his inclinations. Certainly under Antoninus Pius, who, in his own noble words, chose rather 'to save the life of one citizen than to slay a thousand foes', persecutions were local outbreaks, the details of which may, possibly, never have come before the emperor until after the issue. But the martyrdoms of Polycarp and his companions in Smyrna, the great dread which we see haunting the pages of the *Shepherd* of Hermas, the execution in Rome by the prefect Lollius Urbicus of Ptolemaeus and Lucius, show that the peace of the Church was often broken, in spite of the *Apologies* by which Justin, Quadratus and others sought to procure rest for the persecuted. If the surmise of Harnack be correct, the rescript of Antoninus Pius to the Diet ($Kοινόν$) of Asia is itself a witness, not so much to toleration – this is a later Christian interpolation – as to the irregular persecutions that ever and anon broke out in the cities of the East, as well as in Greece and Thrace. Disorder of this sort Pius was determined to put down, as we see from his letter to 'the Larissaeans, Thessalonians, Athenians, and all Greeks'.

The presence of Marcus Aurelius among the persecutors of the Church must ever prove a matter of astonishment and regret. That the one ruler of men who at first blush realizes to the full Plato's dream of the philosopher on the throne should be the hard taskmaster of the followers of Jesus is one of the ironies of history. No doubt part of our surprise arises from a false estimate of the reign of Marcus Aurelius. Historians have too often been misled by the panegyrics of the philosophers who crowded his court, and wrote the record of his rule. In some respects his reign was successful. His laws on behalf of the slave, the child, and the orphan mark the rise in the world of a new moral consciousness, to which, however, Marcus Aurelius was not the first to appeal. Nevertheless, as Schiller has shown us, the reign of the great thinker was, on the whole, a dismal failure, marked by incapacity, and dogged by continual disaster. 'Marcus, partly because he was a good Stoic, was a very bad emperor'. The puzzle further vanishes when we cease to look at Marcus Aurelius from a Christian standpoint, which he would have been the last to understand. Nevertheless, the strange vision of one 'the very dust of whose thoughts was gold', whose soul soared to heights of resignation to the divine will given to few even among the saints of God, as the deliberate persecutor of 'the bond-servants of Jesus Christ', leads us to pause for a moment that we may contrast the doctrine of renunciation as proclaimed by the Christian and the Stoic emperor.

The religion of Marcus Aurelius, which may briefly be described as ethical Calvinism, is undoubtedly founded, as that of Epectetus before him, upon uncomplaining submission to the will of God as the law of the whole universe. For him renunciation must be complete; we must, as Epictetus urged, 'desire nothing too much,' but – and herein lies the difference between Marcus Aurelius and the Christian – this renunciation is without germ of hope either for the individual or society. With Marcus Aurelius renunciation is something essentially Eastern rather than Christian; the sweeping, as by a wintry torrent, of this poor human life into the eternal vortex of the 'universal substance'; the passing from a troubled consciousness into the dreamless life of the God, or 'Logos', 'the governing intelligence', who directs all. For Marcus Aurelius immortality is meaningless; what is the atom of consciousness amid the endless flux of cyclic change, 'that one and all which we name Cosmos', but which is all 'little, changeable, perishable', that man should dream of permanence? For him nature is abosolute, merciless as death, unalterably fixed and ordered. Marcus Aurelius, just because he has no belief in the existence of real evil in the best of all predestined worlds, has no yearning for all that to the Christian is contained in the idea of heaven – that opportunity for completing the incomplete, for making life's crooked straight. The last word of renunciation is for the Stoic emperor a rayless negation, at the best a great uncertainty; for him life is but a moment of consciousness that comes to the surface of the stream of infinite and endless mutation. 'After fame is oblivion'; after death, as best, the soul shall be received back into 'the seminal principle of the universe'—

> We are such stuff
> As dreams are made of, and our little life
> Is rounded by a sleep.

His is the renunciation both of feeling and hope, necessarily passing into despair of the spiritual possibilities of human nature. Thus with Marcus Aurelius renunciation becomes a hopeless concentration upon present duty, for whose sake all else must be put aside. It is magnificent – in some respects the most magnificent flight of the unaided human soul. None the less it is not so much renunciation as despair. But for the Christian the basis of renunciation is hope, both for himself and society. He ever objectifies, if we may so put it, the cause of his self-discipline. The likeness to God is the incentive to his purification; the city of God descending from heaven like a bride is the vision that nerves him for every form of self-sacrifice. But this city of God, or realized Kingdom of Heaven, that organized ideal in which lay the strongest appeal of the new religion, by its very nature utterly subversive of the established order as it then existed, had little meaning for the absoluteness of Stoic individualism.

The student who remembers these things will understand the antipathy of Marcus Aurelius to Christianity. The heroism of the Christian martyr, with his delusion of a golden hereafter, seemed to him, as to

Epictetus his master, based on folly, and an illustration merely of 'Galilean obstinacy'. He is probably contrasting it with the true courage which men display when, in accordance with 'Stoic teaching', they anticipate Nature and seek death by their own suicide. The dread of another world in all its forms he classed with 'superstition'. For those who yielded to this delusion, whether in its nobler or in its baser forms, he decreed banishment or the loss of all their rights.

Moreover, Marcus Aurelius, for whom the Roman tradition had become a dogma, saw in the Christians the great obstacle to the revival of the national religion in a Stoic and eclectic form. He found no difficulty in incorporating in his religion both the popular mythology and rites and the tenets of the philosopher. On the commencement of his war with the Marcomanni, his slaughter of victims was so great that in the popular skits of the day the white cattle lodged a complaint that his final victory would entail their annihilation. From the Christians alone did he meet with a resistance as obstinate as, in his opinion, it was senseless. The philosopher, whatever his private opinions, kept his countenance and fell in with the current ritual. Not so with the untutored Galileans.

But whatever the cause, the fact itself cannot be gainsaid that Christian blood flowed more freely under Marcus Aurelius than at any previous date, with the possible exception of Domitian. Wholesale slaughters in the amphitheatre of Lyons, the martyrdom of Justin and his companions at Rome, of the seven men and five women at Scili, of Namphano and Miggin, Suname and Lucitas – harsh Punic names, written, however, in the Lamb's Book of Life – at Madaura, near Carthage, are sufficient evidence, though but fragmentary and incomplete, of the widespread persecution of the Christians. For the details of these persecutions, the cruelty with which they were executed, we must not hold Marcus Aurelius responsible. He administered an empire a dozen times as large as France; details were necessarily left to local officers. But the emperor decided the general policy; and in this sense the noblest soul of the ancient world became a strenuous persecutor, who did not, it is true, initiate a new antagonism to Christianity so much as carry out more strictly, and in a different spirit, the existing penal code. If it be said that for an emperor there was no choice, we may reply that the evidence proves that Marcus Aurelius was not so careful as Trajan and Hadrian in insisting that in all persecutions the magistrate and not the mob should lead. Moreover, there are clear indications throughout his reign of an active pursuit of the Christians by the magistrates, a return to the procedure discouraged by Trajan and Hadrian.

Marcus Aurelius was succeeded by the worthless Commodus.

Throughout his reign the Church enjoyed an unaccustomed peace; in part because of the influence of his mistress, Marcia, who, if not a Christian herself, had sympathy with the new religion; more perhaps because of an easy-going indifference to causes of disturbance which to more strenuous rulers had seemed of the highest moment. His whole sympathies were with Eastern religions, Mithraism especially, rather than with old national faiths. Shortly after his accession the policy of persecution was stopped, while many of those condemned by Marcus to the mines of Sardinia were released, including the famous, or infamous, pope Callistus. The Church grew mightily, and in Rome many of the upper classes and of the court attached themselves to the new faith with their whole households.

V

With the dawn of the third century we enter upon a new era in the history of persecution. Hitherto, as we have shown, the suppression of Christianity, though the rule of the Empire, had been a matter of police regulation, carried out locally in a somewhat fitful manner, rather than pursued systematically on definite instructions from headquarters. The rescripts of Trajan and Hadrian were not directed against Christianity as an organization, but dealt with certain details of executive administration exactly in the same way as if the question had been one of brigandage, or illegal trades unions. Of any consciousness that Christianity as a Church was in itself a danger to the State, except in the sense that all wrong-doers are dangerous, we see as yet little sign or proof. The existing hatred of the new religion was more a matter of personal feeling than a question of high politics, though the outbreak of local persecutions could not fail to come under the ken of the emperors, and to receive their sanction or regulation.

But all this was now changed. In the early years of the third century we see the emperors realizing, dimly and imperfectly at first, that the Church which their predecessors had persecuted was no mere body of anarchists to be rooted out wherever necessary, but a rival organization of growing strength, whose increase in numbers and unity of administration made its suppression, if possible, or if not its adoption as a 'tolerated religion', a political necessity. By the middle of the century this consciousness of a great struggle and danger had become so clear and definite, that we see organized efforts on the part of the more energetic rulers to crush out the Church by the use of all the resources of the State. The police measures of the Antonines gave place to a civil war without quarter. But, unlike all other civil wars, only one side was armed. Strange to say, this was the side that was ultimately defeated. On the one hand were the immense resources of the Empire centralized in one supreme will; on the other the passive resistance of enthusiasts making these resources useless. Nor were the forces of paganism material only. She called to her aid a succession of able philosophers and controversialists, Celsus, Porphyry, Hierocles, Theotecnus, and others, who sought in various ways to entrench the established religion, and to destroy with their criticisms the claims of the new faith. Paganism itself became more serious and spiritual as she realized the mortal nature of the struggle.

The student should note the apparent unequalness of the conflict. To some extent he may be misled in this matter by the glowing rhetoric of the apologists. If we were to accept the statements of Tertullian and other Fathers, the conquest of Christianity would not be so marvellous as it must ever seem to the sober historian; for the Fathers write as if the famous sentence 'Veni, vidi, vici' could be applied literally to the Church. They leave us with the impression that nothing could withstand the onward sweep of the hosts of God, and yet, somehow or other, Christians were almost powerless against the persecutor; two positions one or other of which must be incorrect. Irenaeus boasts of 'many nations among the barbarians who believe, having salvation written on their hearts by the Spirit, without ink or paper'. He is followed by Tertullian. 'Places inaccessible to Rome,' cries the orator, 'have yielded to Christ' – he is speaking of the spread of the gospel in Britain – and dwells on the 'remote peoples, provinces, and islands which we know not nor can enumerate', which have embraced the faith. In another place he threatens the State with the dangers that arise from the universality of the Christians—

If we wanted to play the part of avowed enemies, should we be lacking in numbers or resources? Do the Parthians themselves, or any nation, however great, which is yet restricted to one country and dwells within its own boundaries, outnumber one that is spread all over the world? We are but of yesterday, yet we have filled the places you frequent – cities, villages, markets, the camp itself, town councils, the palace, the senate, the forum. All we have left you is your temples. . . . Nearly all the citizens of nearly all your cities are Christians.

Such passages could be multiplied, without, however, increasing their value as evidence. For all this was little more than rhetoric, the result to some extent of millenarian or parousian conceptions. It was necessary for the Second Advent that the gospel should first have been preached in every land. At the close of the first century we find Clement of Rome maintaining that this condition has been fulfilled by St. Paul so far as the Empire was concerned. A few years later Ignatius talks of 'bishops settled in the utmost corners of the earth'. By the middle of the second century, as we have seen, the Church had persuaded herself that her warfare was accomplished. The *Shepherd* of Hermas speaks 'of all the nations under heaven called by the name of the Son of God', while Justin Martyr claimed that 'there is not a single race of human beings, barbarians, Greeks or nomads, where prayers in the name of Jesus the crucified are not offered up'. Hope was mistaken for accomplished fact. Imagination, untrammelled by statistics, soared above mere details. Such glorious optimism is characteristic of Christianity. To the Church, as to her Master, time is but an accident. She sees already of the travail of her soul, and is satisfied. The 'not yet' of the cautious critic (Heb. 2: 8, 9) is more than neutralized by the vision of the triumphant King.

As a matter of fact, Christianity in the opening years of the second century was still but a feeble minority when compared with the vast masses and resources of heathenism, of less importance probably than Judaism. The statement of Origen is explicit: 'Many people, not only barbarians, but even in the Empire, have not yet heard the word of Christ.' Elsewhere he speaks of the Christians 'as at present a mere handful of people', in comparison with the Empire. No statistics of Christianity are available; for that matter, we are ignorant of the population of the Empire itself. But the lines of proof are sufficient to show that only here and there, in a few great towns such as Rome, Antioch, and Alexandria, in still fewer country districts, chiefly in Asia Minor, was Christianity at all strong numerically speaking. In most regions of the Empire it was still non-existent; while the countryside, even in the neighbourhood of Christian cities, was almost wholly pagan. The extension of Christianity in the main coincided with the extension throughout the world of Hellenism; its lines of development for the most part were along the great trade routes. In many places we find that the Christians belong almost wholly to the floating population, commercial or otherwise.

But though a minority, the emperors saw that the Christians were a dangerous minority, daily growing, moreover, in numbers and power. Between the years 200 and 250 Christianity seems to have made rapid advance; while the increasing unity of its organization, under the pressure of Gnostic heresies, made it the more dangerous. The insight of Decius was correct when he declared that he would rather see a rival emperor in the field than another pope in Rome. His outburst was due perhaps to his hearing that Pope Fabian had actually substituted for the fourteen civil districts of Rome a division into seven of his own. Moreover, the Christians were exceedingly wealthy; sobriety and character had produced their usual results. The confiscation of their public and private property would provide relief for the impending bankruptcy of the State.

We do well to note that the conflict of the Church and the Empire synchronized with a new conception on the part of the Empire of its own constitution. Hitherto citizenship had been restricted to a few, chiefly Italians, the inhabitants of certain special colonies, or the successful legions. By an edict of Caracalla the name and privileges of Romans was conceded to all the free inhabitants of the Empire. Thus a Catholic Church faced a world-wide Empire.

The first emperor to realize the new conditions and to attempt the suppression of the Church was the able Septimius Severus. At the outset of his reign Severus had treated the Christians with a certain degree of leniency; he had received benefit during dangerous illness from a Christian slave, who had anointed him with oil. He allowed Christians in his court. The nurse as well as the tutor of his son Caracalla were Christians. According to one account, on his entry into Rome after his victory over his rival Albinus, Severus protected certain well-known Christians from the anger of the mob. But in the beginning of the year 201, on his journey through Palestine to Egypt, Severus, alarmed by the rapid growth of the new religion, and the increasing menace of its tone, possibly resenting also certain indiscretions in the army, found it necessary to take active measures against Christianity. He ordered that no one should be allowed to become a proselyte to Judaism, and applied the same to the Church, a needless edict this last – except in so far as it was designed to correct his previous toleration – when we remember that it was still illegal to be a Christian at all. This warning given, Severus in the following year passed to the severest measures of repression, though his persecution, which lasted until the second year of Caracalla, was chiefly confined to the East, and to North Africa. According to Eusebius, the 'great theatre of God for those heroic wrestlers was Alexandria', where, among others, Leonides, the father of Origen, 'obtained the crown'. The student of Tertullian, our chief Western authority for the relations of State and Church under Septimus Severus, especially of the address which at this time (211–12) he presented to Scapula, the prefect of Africa, will be at no loss to discover the cause of persecution. Every sentence of the Apologist breathes defiance, or heaps contempt upon the customs of heathenism. Nor were the pagans backward in their hatred and slander of the Christians.

With the death of Septimius Severus at York (4 Feb. 211) and the succession of his worthless sons, the Church for a time enjoyed comparative rest. In part this was due to a succession of foreign emperors with no hereditary attachment to the Roman national religion; half-mad Syrian voluptuaries like Elagabalus, who dreamed of a universal religion to be obtained by the fusion of all other faiths, Christianity included, into one great system in which the sun, under the form of a black conical stone, should be the central object of worship. In the cousin and successor of Elagabalus, another Syrian of nobler mould who assumed the title of Alexander Severus, we see the same syncretism in a higher form. In his private oratory (*lararium*) he erected, so gossip ran, a statue of Jesus, side by side with those of Abraham, Orpheus, and Apollonius of Tyana. Many of high rank in his court were believers. He had ordered, it was said, the Golden Rule to be written up in his palace. In a lawsuit between the Christians and a company of victuallers for the possession of a piece of ground in Rome, Alexander awarded the site to the Christians. 'Better', he said, 'that the land should be devoted to the worship of God in any form than that it should be handed over for the uses of cookships.' When his mother, the Empress Julia Mamaea, passed through Antioch, she sent for Origen:

With her he staid some time, exhibiting innumerable matters calculated to promote the glory of the Lord, and to evince the excellence of divine instruction. After this he returned to his accustomed duties.

But beneath this apparent calm there was the growing dread and hostility of paganism. We see this, as Gibbon has suggested, in those counsels of persecution which Dion Cassius, who composed his history during this reign, has put into the mouth of Maecenas, and which were 'most probably intended for the use of his master'. We have a further illustration in the fact that it was at this time that the lawyers codified the existing laws against Christianity.

With the murder of Alexander Severus and his mother at Mainz persecution once more broke out. The very success of the Christians proved their undoing. Hitherto they had met for worship in private houses, or in the cemeteries of their dead; now they were permitted to purchase sites, to erect churches. Their bishops already possessed an influence by no means limited to their congregations. The upper clergy, therefore, were the first to feel the hatred of Maximin the Thracian, a gigantic barbarian, ignorant of Latin, the first who sat on the throne of the Caesars. Many perished in the massacre of the friends of Alexander with which this tyrant began his short disastrous reign. In Rome Pope Pontian and Hippolytus were exiled to Sardinia. There the pope was beaten to death. The short papacy of his successor Anteros shows the bitterness of the persecution. His execution may have been due to the 'diligence' with which he 'collected from the notaries the records of the martyrs'. In

Cappadocia and Pontus, where an earthquake had irritated the people against the Christians, the persecution was especially severe. But Maximin's oppression of the Church, though widespread, was not so much systematic as a part of the general horror of his rule. Public opinion, usually cast against the Christians, in this case refused to side with the tyrant. Maximin's purging his court of Christians was afterwards copied by Decius and Valerian. There was, in fact, no alternative. The position had become such that an emperor must either drive out the Christians from his palace, or allow himself to be dominated by them.

Under the Emperor Philip the Arabian, the Christians enjoyed for five brief years, not only rest, but a measure of protection and encouragement. The growth of the Church in all ranks and classes was remarkable. Everywhere the Christians felt the need of larger buildings to replace the older oratories. How great was the peace of the Church we see from the prevalence in later days of the idea that the head of the State had become a convert to the new faith. Nor was the idea dispelled by the magnificence with which Philip celebrated on the thousandth anniversary of the foundation of Rome the secular games, the great religious rites of Rome (21 April 248). Perhaps the suspicion was due to the fact that he had not visited with stern punishment the Christians, the more rigid of whom would abstain from this great festival of national pride. But with the fall of Philip the Empire set itself resolutely to the task of crushing out the Christians.

The movement for reform – for such it seemed to the pagan party – had its centre in the army, the one branch of the body politic least influenced by Christianity, where the old manners and discipline still retained to some extent their power. Decius, an able Pannonian soldier whose virtues 'ranked him with the ancients', conscious of the weakness of the Empire, and its growing inability to bear its burdens, attempted to restore strength by striking at what he considered a prime cause of disunion. He determined to enforce universal observance of the national religion. This, with most Romans, he deemed to be catholic enough for all tastes. Thus he would put an end to social and moral confusion. For this purpose he allied himself with the Senate, the home of all heathen and conservative reactions. To strengthen his hand he revived in the person of Valerian the office of censor. For outbreaks of local hatred he would substitute a universal and organized scheme. With Goths, Franks, and Persians threatening to inundate the Empire, no more inopportune time could have been chosen for thus estranging an influential and numerous section of his people. But Decius was a political idealist rather than a practical statesman.

Early in 250 Decius published his edict against Christianity. He commanded provincial governors and magistrates, assisted where necessary by a commission of notable citizens, to see to it that all men sacrificed to the gods and to the genius of the emperor on a certain fixed day. Part of the ritual consisted also in tasting the sacrifices, as we see from the story of the apostate bishop Euctemon. Special attention was to be paid to the officers of the Church, under the belief 'that if he removed all the heads the entire fabric would dissolve'. But Decius did not contemplate extermination. At first capital punishment, except in the case of bishops, does not seem to have been authorized, though banishment and torture might be employed to break the stubborn. The emperor was persuaded that if the magistrates only put sufficient pressure upon the Christians, they would abandon their faith. He had grounds for this belief in the recent addition to the Church of thousands of converts who had rather changed their creeds than their characters, self-indulgent effeminate men, painted women, and ambitious clergy, upon whose worldly lives the persecution seemed to some to be a fitting judgement. Such rushed eagerly to the magistrates to obtain their *libelli*, or certificates of sacrifice, and when the days of persecution were over were as eager to be readmitted to the Church.

There was hardly a province of the Empire in which the violence of the storm was not felt, and which did not obtain its bede-roll of martyrs. For the faithful who refused to sell their Lord were hunted out, banished, their property confiscated, they themselves exposed to insults, outrage, torture, death. The confessors, it is true, were more numerous than the martyrs, for the object of Decius was by prison and torture to produce recantation. A measure of forbearance also was shown to the humbler Christians, unless indeed it be that no steps were taken by the Church to record their sufferings. In Rome itself the policy of striking down the officials rather than the members was strictly carried out. On 20 January 250 Pope Fabian was executed, and so severe was the persecution that for fourteen months no successor could safely be appointed. But 'the Church held firmly to the faith, though some fell through fear'. The proportion of brave women among the confessors, of whom, alas! we know nothing but the names, is remarkable. Two highborn Persians, Abdon and Sennen, as well as two Armenians, Parthenius and Calocerus, witness by their deaths at Rome to the spread of the gospel. They were perhaps fugitives from persecution elsewhere, for, strange to say, Rome, with its large Christian Church, seems to have been almost the safest place in the Empire, at any rate after the departure of Decius. We see this in the arrival of no less than sixty-five confessors in one ship, who were met at the harbour by Numeria and Candida, two girls who attempted to atone for their weakness in the day of trial by ministering to the needy.

But the severity of the persecution was most experienced in Africa. In Carthage the more part of the Church apostatized, 'spurring one another on with encouraging words, and in turn pledging each other in the cup of death'. Among the weaklings were some of the clergy, who probably missed the presence and support of their bishop, Cyprian. Certain bishops also denied the faith. But many, among them women not a few, were faithful unto death. We hear of seventeen, the comrades of a confessor called Lucian, who died together in prison of hunger and thirst.

In Egypt the persecution in Alexandria, begun under Philip, was renewed. Here also, as at Carthage, there were many backsliders. 'Others, however, were firm and blessed pillars of the Lord', among them an old man, Julian by name. As his gout would not allow him to walk, he was carried to the stake on a camel, amid the jeers of the mob. We read also of Dioscuros, a boy of fifteen, 'who was neither persuaded by words nor constrained by tortures'. Five Christian soldiers, one of them a veteran, were standing on duty by the tribunal. Noticing signs of wavering in a prisoner, they made vigorous signs to him to stand firm. On being observed, 'they ran up to the tribunal and declared that they were Christians'. Dionysius, the great bishop of Alexandria, escaped. For four days he lay hid in his own home while the police searched high and low. He then decided on flight, and was captured by the soldiers. But as one of his friends, a certain Timothy, who happened to have escaped, was flying along in great distress, 'he met a peasant, who asked the cause of his haste. On hearing the same the peasant went his way, for he was going to a marriage feast'. On his arrival the countryman told the story to the others, some of whom, apparently, were Christians:

These, forthwith, with a single impulse arose and came as quickly as possible with a rush and a shout upon us – (Dionysius himself tells the story) – The soldiers immediately took to flight, and the peasants came upon us, lying as we were upon the bare bedsteads. I indeed, God knows, thought at first that they were robbers. Lying there on my bed, naked save for a linen cloth, I offered them the rest of my clothes. But they told me to get up and get away as quickly as possible.

As Dionysius seemed unwilling to flee, his friends set him on an unsaddled ass and carried him off to the desert.

In Syria and Asia Minor the persecution raged fitfully. The great theologian Origen, who was now in his sixty-eighth year, was racked to the fourth hole. Only by the ingenuity of his judge was he saved from succumbing to his tortures, from the effects of which, however, he died at Tyre in 254. In Pontus, as in Carthage and Alexandria, the laxity of the authorities was such that Gregory the Wonder-worker succeeded in escaping. Decius was too busy with his campaigns in Gaul and Pannonia to see that the magistrates carried out his instructions. But here and there the prisons were filled, and the torturers busy. In Smyrna 'the lusty athlete' Pionius and his companions witnessed the good confession, in spite of the apostasy of their bishop, Euctemon. But Babylas of Antioch and Alexander of Jerusalem proved by their deaths that not all the hierarchy were cowards.

The persecution of Decius, happily, was of but brief duration. The barbarians providentially came to the assistance of the Church, as also in the later crisis under Valerian. Even before the death of Decius at the hands of the Goths in the marshes of the Dobrudsha (August, 251), the pressure of his foes had wrung from him a measure of rest for the Christians. We see this in their election in the previous March of Pope Cornelius. In the following year the persecution was renewed by Gallus, through whose treachery Decius had perished. The occasion was found in the terror inspired by a pestilence which swept from end to end of the Roman world. Expiatory sacrifices to avert the anger of the gods were ordered to be offered throughout the Empire. 'We see,' wrote the African bishops, 'that a second season of attack is drawing near.' But the treacherous Gallus was a foe far inferior to the virtuous Decius; while the Church, purified by its trials and repentance, was stronger than in the former persecution. The attack failed, though we know that for a time the persecution extended over Italy, Africa, and Egypt. In Carthage the mob clamoured for Cyprian to be thrown to the beasts. In Rome Cornelius was banished to Civita Vecchia, where shortly afterwards he died. His successor Lucius was no sooner appointed than he too was banished. But the murder of Gallus by his own troops put an end to the struggle. Lucius was allowed to return to Rome, where shortly afterwards he died in peace. The secret of Rome's success in the past lay in her continuity of policy. Now her growing weakness was shown by the way in which successive emperors cancelled the measures taken against the Christians by their predecessors.

VI

The accession of the aged censor Valerian (Aug. 253), a noble Roman of rigid life and unswerving fidelity of duty, but of somewhat irresolute character, soon issued in the renewal of the struggle. The reign of Valerian – who at an early date associated with himself his son Gallienus – in spite of the many virtues of the emperor, was one of the most unfortunate in the annals of Rome. On its frontiers Franks, Alemanni, Marcomanni, and Goths in all directions were pressing in upon the dying Empire. For fifteen years a great plague ravaged its provinces, carrying off in Alexandria and other cities more than half the population. Seasons of scorching drought were followed by terrific tornadoes. A debased coinage led to financial disaster. Famine, earthquakes, and huge tidal waves completed the ruin.

In the early months of his reign, though the laws of Decius were still in force, the Christians were not molested. Valerian was too busy attempting to reduce the chaos in the State to order, and in providing for the defence of the frontiers, to meddle with the Church. There are grounds for believing that at first he viewed the Christians with some favour. He allowed Pope Lucius to return from his exile. 'His house was in truth a congregation (ἐκκλησία) of the Lord'; so numerous were the Christians in his palace that the 'Caesariani' are expressly singled out for punishment in his second edict of persecution. But now there came a change; to some extent due to the constant calamities of the Empire and the superstition of the people, more, perhaps, because of the growing influence upon Valerian of Macrianus, one of the chief members of his court, the head of the magi of Egypt. Through this man's machinations Valerian began a terrible persecution of the Church. In the summer of 257 he issued an edict specially directed against the bishops and priests. These the magistrates must seize and compel, under the alternative of banishment, to offer the outer signs of conformity, as in the persecution of Decius. The decree also forbade, under pain of death, the assembling together of the Christians for worship, or their further use of their cemeteries.

Few details of the effect of this rescript have come down to us. At Rome, for reasons which are now lost, the Christians succeeded to a large extent in evading it. In Carthage it led to the banishment of Cyprian to Curubis. In some places where the Christians continued to hold their meetings they were arrested in large numbers, and condemned to death or to the mines. Among these last were nine Numidian bishops, to whom Cyprian wrote a letter of consolation from his place of exile. Dionysius of Alexandria was deported to Kephron, a wretched village in the desert, where the pagans attacked the Christian aliens with stones. Recantations were few, if any, though in some districts the edict was rigidly enforced. The worldling and coward had been driven out of the Church by the fire and sword of Decius.

A year later (Aug. 258) Valerian, conscious of the failure of his first edict, published a second of increased severity. This rescript was possibly the result of the reports he had received from his lieutenants, most of whom had been present at the emperor's brilliant levée at Byzantium in the summer of 258. Valerian deemed that the time was opportune for his reform, inasmuch as he had recently won several successes on the Rhine and Danube. He determined to strike at the clergy. Wherever found, of whatever grade, the penalty for the clergy was death, without the avail of recantation. The leaders among the laity, senators, and knights, were condemned to the same fate, but with the option of backsliding. Noble ladies were sentenced to be banished. Members of the court were to be sent in chains to work as slaves on the imperial estates. No mention is made of the treatment of humble Christians. Valerian hoped that the sheep thus left without shepherds would come back to the true fold without being worried.

The first victim of the rescript was Pope Xystus II. In spite of the edict, he had assembled the faithful in a little oratory, or *schola*, in the cemetery of Praetextatus – not in the catacomb of Callixtus; that was too well known to the authorities for safety. The soldiers rushed in, the pope was hurried before the judge, and of course condemned. He was brought back to the cemetery and put to death as he sat in his episcopal chair, together with four of his deacons. Four days later the same fate overtook other deacons and readers, among them the famous St. Lawrence. In the provinces Cyprian at Carthage, Agapius and Secundinus at Cirta, Bishop Fructuosus of Tarragona, Lucius and Montanus, Marianus and James, Leo of Patara, and many others, suffered torture and death, of a few of whom we know but the names, of most possess no record at all.

But the fall of Valerian was at hand. The legions, enfeebled by the plague, distracted by civil wars, were powerless to hurl back the seething hordes that pushed over the frontiers. In the West the Alemanni ravaged Italy up to the walls of Ravenna (259), while Dacia was torn from the Empire by the Goths, who thence pursued their ravages across the Bosphorus into Asia. In the East Valerian, in attempting, probably, to prevent the junction of Goths and Persians, was defeated by the latter under Shapûr (Sapor) and betrayed to the enemy. For six years the unfortunate emperor was dragged about at the stirrup of his conqueror, robed in purple but weighed down with chains. When at length death came to his release, his skin was dyed with vermilion, stuffed with straw, and hung up in unavenged derision in a Persian temple.

Valerian was succeeded by Gallienus, a clever man without character or real patriotism. He took no steps to procure his father's release; the revolt of provinces was accepted with a smile. Usurpers sprang up everywhere; the Thirty Tyrants reduced the Empire to chaos. For all these things Gallienus, cynic and voluptuary, cared nothing. But whether from indifference, rare statesmanship, the influence of his wife Salonina, or the philosophical syncretism which attached him to Plotinus and the Neoplatonists, Gallienus determined to put an end to the sanguinary struggle between Christianity and the State. The Empire was bleeding to death; one wound, at any rate, might be staunched. So Gallienus issued an edict of toleration, restoring to the Church their confiscated basilicas, reopening their cemeteries, and guaranteeing freedom of worship. In the East the social disorders led to some delay; but finally, both in East and West, Christianity thus became definitely enrolled as a *religio licita*, and so continued until the persecution of Diocletian. How strong was now their legal position is shown by the incident of the appeal of the Christians of Antioch against their bishop Paul of Samosata to the Emperor Aurelian, the issue of which was the recognition by Aurelian of the rights of the Roman section in the Church to the buildings. The edict of Milan fifty-three years later did little more than restore the legislation of Gallienus.

The execution of Xystus in the catacombs tempts us to interrupt our story that we may explain more fully a matter intimately bound up with the martyrs from the days of the Apostles onward. We allude to their tombs. The reader familiar with the savage fanaticism which tossed the ashes of Hus into the Rhine, tore up Wyclif from his grave at Lutterworth and cast the dust into the Swift – two only out of many illustrations – may wonder that the Roman governors allowed the burial of the martyrs at all. But in this matter pagan Rome must not be compared with the horrible vindictiveness of the mediaeval Inquisition. To the heathen judge, unlike the Council of Constance or Bishop Fleming of Lincoln, the dust even of the criminals was sacred, and must be delivered up to the relatives or friends. Even a Nero dare not tamper with that right, and there is nothing in itself more probable than that a Roman matron of wealth should be allowed to claim and bury the bodies of St. Paul and St. Peter in her own freehold. What was more, the place of burial by that very fact became sacred (*religiosus*) in the eyes of the law, a place as inviolable as the holiest temple. Thus the tombs of the martyrs for instance of St. Peter on the Aurelian Way, of St. Paul on the Ostian, whether above ground or below, would be built with as much impunity as the mole of Hadrian or the mausoleum of Augustus, and with rights of access to the tombs fully secured, even in case of the sale of the property. Thus the law itself, by the safety it insured for the graves of the martyrs, assisted by the reverence of the Church and the desire of the faithful to be buried side by side with the holy dead, was the real force that dug out the catacombs. For the catacombs were not, as was once supposed, disused quarries which trembling Christians secretly adapted for their own purposes. They were galleries deliberately constructed by several generations of Christians at great cost by sextons (*fossores*) recognized as servants of the Church, and with an evident consciousness of security and right. In this, as in so much else, the Church was but the lineal descendant of Judaism, whose catacombs at Rome, undoubtedly anterior to Christianity, furnished to some extent the model of all later developments. We have an illustration of this in the fact that of the fifteen bishops of Rome who preceded Zephyrinus all but Clement and Alexander were buried 'hard by the body of St. Peter'. We cannot imagine that the imperial police were ignorant of this recognized burial-place of the leaders of a sect officially classed with cut-throats and anarchists. Nevertheless, no interference was attempted. In the third century Zephyrinus changed the tomb of the popes to the cemetery which he had provided, possibly because the little plot on the Vatican was full. But the thirteen bishops of Rome buried in this new catacomb were perfectly safe, despite the persecutions of Decius, Valerian, and Diocletian, of which, in fact, some had been the victims.

These burial-places were at first known by the names of the owner of the freehold, not only for legal reasons, but because the familiar galleries were really developments that radiated out from these private sepulchral areas. Only in later times, and then by no means commonly, were they called from some famous saint whose tomb they contained. Furthermore, in every case, by Roman law, they were without the walls. No corpse save that of a vestal virgin was allowed to be buried within the city itself. But this very fact gave them a certain privacy, which, added to their inviolability, enabled the catacombs to become a safe meeting-place for worship in times of persecutions. The provision of these cemeteries was left at first to private generosity. But early in the third century the Church took advantage of the laws relating to burial clubs to purchase cemeteries, the freehold of which was vested in the bishop or other official. In this very development we mark one of the notes of Christianity. Pagan cemeteries were usually restricted to the members of a particular *familia*, but in the brotherhood of Christ they were open to the community of the faithful.

From the earliest days of the City jurisdiction in all matters of burial, including the responsibility for guarding inviolability, was left to the pontiffs (*pontifices*). Every transference of a body, even simple repairs of the tomb, had first to obtain their sanction. If this was secured (and in such matters the pontiffs were lenient), the transference of a Christian from one tomb to another became a legal act, in spite of the fact that Christianity itself was illegal. This will illustrate a most interesting event which took place towards the close of the first year of persecution under Valerian, and which may well have led to the immediate issue of his second rescript. On 29 June 258, a few weeks before the martyrdom of

Xystus, the bodies of St. Peter and St. Paul were transferred from the places where hitherto they had rested to another place 'in Catacumbas'. Whether this was done for the greater security in time of persecution of the precious remains, in dread lest the heathen should attack their well-known shrines, or from some other cause – for instance, the need of repairing the tombs – we cannot tell. If carried out ostentatiously with the pontiffs' consent, it was a dangerous step, as it marked out the men who took part in it, Xystus included; if done secretly at night, it could not fail to be reported by the police, and thus give Valerian reason for striking harder at such daring law-breakers.

We have said the cemeteries were guarded by custom and legislation. But in times of persecution the mob occasionally defied the law, the more easily as Christians condemned for '*majestas*' were really outside its pale. In the great outbreak at Lyons the persecutors cast the ashes of the martyrs into the Rhone—

in order, as they said, that they may not have hope in a resurrection, in the strength of which they despise dangers and go with joy to meet death (*Euseb. HE* v 1).

Outrages upon the tombs of the hated anarchists might also at times be committed with impunity by reason of the sympathetic blindness of the police. This will account for the frequent appeals to the fears of the law-breaker which we find on Christian graves. Thus on a tomb at Milan we read: 'May the wrath of God and of His Christ fall on him who dares to disturb the peace of our sleep'. But the Christian did not as a rule so openly expose his faith. In Phrygia, for instance, he used a phrase that would not jar on pagan susceptibilities: 'the violator shall account to the God'. Underground vaults were naturally less exposed to such lawless deeds, and, so far as we know, until the persecutions of the third century the sanctity of the catacombs was scrupulously respected by the responsible magistrates.

De Rossi was of opinion that the first attempts to make the catacombs secret may be dated as due to the persecutions of Septimius Severus. Tertullian speaks of the Christians as being arrested 'in their secret gathering-places'; while in Carthage the cry arose, 'No burial-grounds for the Christians'. The edict of Valerian and the arrest of Xystus II led to many devices – irregular and circuitous passages, concealed ways of entrance through the sand quarries (*arenariae*) which often lay adjacent, steps destroyed so that without a ladder the intruder was helpless, and the like – for the better guarding of their cemeteries. But, in spite of all precautions, the catacombs were probably the scene of many surprises and not a few tragedies. On one occasion, if we may quote a doubtful tale of

Gregory of Tours, when the Christians were seen to enter, the passage was hastily walled up, so that they were all buried alive. Whatever be the truth of Gregory's tale, such a fate for the Christians was probably not unknown.

VII

With the accession of the great Emperor Diocletian (17 September 284), we enter upon the final struggle – the tenth wave, as Christians said, of the great storm. Diocletian's parents had been slaves in the household of the Senator Anulinus; their child refounded the Empire on a new basis, transforming the principate of Augustus into an absolute monarchy. Diocletian's reorganization of the Empire was followed by the concentration of the forces of that Empire against the Church. All was changing; Rome had become almost a provincial city, forced to pay taxes like the rest of the world, of less importance than Milan or Nicomedeia. The old rule of a solitary *imperator* gave place to the tetrarchy of two Augusti and two Caesars; the old provinces had been regrouped as dioceses. Nothing would have been more natural than that Diocletian should have done what Constantine found it necessary to do later – to consolidate his other changes by a change in the national religion. But the time for that was not yet. In spite of himself, Diocletian was driven into persecution.

The conflict with the Church did not break out immediately. In his early years, Diocletian had somewhat favoured Christianity. His wife Prisca and his daughter Valeria were catechumens, though as yet they had made no open confession of faith. So also were many of his court officials, among them the influential eunuchs Dorotheus and Gorgonius, as also Lucian the chamberlain. As his earlier acts prove, by temper Diocletian was tolerant, inclined to look on all national religions as worthy of patronage. Nevertheless, by his adoption at his accession of the title of Jovius, Diocletian showed his determination to revive and uphold the religion of the Empire. Isolated persecutions here and there in the army show the slumbering forces of hatred; while Eusebius' description of the 'vast congregations of men who flocked to the religion of Christ', and of the 'spacious churches' that were daily being erected, indicate that the death-grip of the two rivals could not long be averted. In Nicomedeia, the capital of Diocletian, the most conspicuous edifice in the city was the great Christian basilica, which towered up on an eminence in full sight of his palace windows. For the Church in every province the last fifty years had been years of remarkable growth. The Empire must determine whether it should maintain the national religion, or allow it to be displaced by the new faith to which the careless Gallienus had granted toleration.

The heathen priests soon found their opportunity, as in the case of Valerian, in the devotion of Diocletian to the rites of divination. The emperor, who was anxiously waiting at Antioch for news of the success of Galerius in his second expedition against the Persians (297), consulted the omens. Victim after victim was sacrificed, but with no result. Then the master of the soothsayers, who had observed some of the court sign themselves with the cross – the familiar remedy of Christian officials for bowing themselves in the house of Rimmon – informed Diocletian: 'There are profane persons here who obstruct the rites.' Diocletian, in a rage, gave orders that all who were present should be made to sacrifice, and sent messages that the same test should be applied to the troops. But his anger soon passed away; for a time nothing further was done. With the success of Galerius, Diocletian celebrated the last triumph which ever swept along the Sacred Way.

Galerius Maximian, in his youth a Dacian neat-herd, was the evil genius of Diocletian. A brave and able soldier, faithful and imbued with his mother Romula's hatred of the Christians, who had angered the old lady by fasting and praying when invited to join her entertainments. After long but secret conferences, Diocletian was induced by Galerius and Hierocles, the President of Bithynia – this last an able controversialist against the Christians – to issue a decree on the feast of Terminalia (23 Feb 303), an appropriate day for the purpose, intended to set a limit or term to the growth of the new society. By this rescript the edict of toleration of Gallienus was repealed, the statutes of Valerian re-enacted. All churches were to be demolished; all sacred books to be burnt – in this last we may surely trace the counsels of Hierocles, who is said to have known the Scriptures by heart – all Christian officials were to be deprived of their civil rights; Christians who were not officials must be reduced to the rank of slaves. Galerius had wished to condemn to the flames all those who declined to sacrifice. Diocletian refused to allow the shedding of blood. He intended to crush out the Church, not rob his empire of citizens. He desired a Test Act, not a measure of extermination. But two fires in the palace within a fortnight – the work of the Christians, said the heathen; a plot of the heathen, retorted the Christians – were skilfully used by Galerius to stir up Diocletian to still greater repression. 'As Diocletian himself used to say, "the best of emperors, no matter how well intentioned, sometimes errs!" ' Persecution, once begun, could not long proceed on methods of rose-water. Prisca and Valeria were compelled to sacrifice; the trusted officials Dorotheus, Gorgonius, and a page named Peter put to death, the first victims of the accusation of incendiarism. Everywhere persecution raged; the Christians were seized; thrust into prisons, burnt, or drowned.

A few months later Diocletian issued a second edict. The immediate reason is unknown, but Diocletian's severe treatment of a revolt at Antioch, if a mad escapade of five hundred soldiers engaged in dredging may be so described, shows that he was nervous of disaffection in one of the centres of the new faith. In Melitene, another stronghold of the Church, there seems also to have been some attempt at rebellion. In Armenia Tiridates (Trdat) the king was known to be a convert to Christianity. So Diocletian deemed it wise to take decided measures. He put into force the chapter in the edict of Valerian hitherto omitted, and ordered the imprisonment of all the clergy.

Throughout the world the passions of the heathen were let loose without restraint. The clergy were seized. Especial search also was made for the Scriptures. Deacons and readers were tortured until they surrendered their copies to the flames. In Asia Minor a town in which the Christians were in a majority was completely wiped out. Only in Britain and Gaul, where Constantius ruled – Spain was in the government of the cruel Datian, an officer of Maximian – was there any safety for the Christians, though even that tolerant emperor deemed it wiser to conform to the letters he had received from Diocletian so far as to destroy their churches. In our own island the Christians, it must be confessed, were but few in numbers, though not without the powerful support of the Empress Helena. To this date we must assign the martyrdom of a young Roman soldier of Verulam, named Alban, who was executed, according to the doubtful story, for harbouring a priest – a defiance both of the edict and of the discipline of the camp.

The effort of the persecutors to stamp out the Scriptures led to some interesting incidents. In many churches the precious manuscripts were hurriedly hidden, so that 'when the officers reached the library the bookshelves were empty'. At Cirta, in consequence, we see the magistrates, with a policeman called Ox (*Bos*), going round from house to house, guided by the bishop's traitor secretaries (19 May 303):

And when they came to the house of Felix the tailor, he brought out five books, and when they came to the house of Projestus, he brought five big and two little books. Victor the schoolmaster brought out two books, and four books of five volumes each (*quiniones quattuor*). Felix the perpetual flamen said to him, 'Bring your Scriptures out; you have more.' Victor the schoolmaster said, 'If I had more I should have brought them.' When they came to the house of Eutychius, who was in the civil service (*Caesariensis*), the flamen said, 'Bring out your books, that you may obey the order.' 'I have none,' he replied. 'Your answer,' said Felix, 'is taken down.' At the house of Coddeo, Coddeo's wife brought out six books. Felix said, 'Look and see if you have not some more.' The woman said, 'I have no more.' So Felix said to policeman Ox, 'Go in and see if she has any more.' Said the policeman, 'I have looked, and found none.'

We hear of one wily bishop, Mensurius of Carthage, who removed all the library of his church, but took care not to leave the shelves bare. He placed thereon a number of heretical works of little value. The pagans fell into the trap and destroyed the poison, while the bishop's library escaped, in spite of certain busybodies who tried to inform the proconsul of the mistake his police had made.

We owe the record of the doings at Cirta to a later inquiry, under Constantine the Great, into the character of certain of the parties concerned. To the same cause we are indebted for another photograph of the times, which deals with the trial, in the year 314, in the vicarial court of Carthage, of Felix, bishop of Autumni, 'for giving his consent to the surrender of the Scriptures'. Caecilian, who had been in office in Autumni in 303 – the year of the persecution – is put into the witness-box. He deposed as follows:—

I had been with Saturninus to Zama over a question of boundaries. When we came back to Autumni, the Christians sent me to the court, to ask, 'Has the imperial decree reached you yet?' I said, 'No; but I have already seen copies of it, and at Zama and Furni I have seen churches destroyed, and books burned, so you may as well be ready to produce whatever books you have. . . .' Shortly afterwards I sent to the house of the accused Bishop Felix. The police brought back word that he was away. . . . So I wrote a letter to the said Bishop Felix.

The letter was handed up, hastily recognized by Caecilian, and then read to the court. It was as follows:—

I hope you are very well. I enclose the signet-ring which the Christians, among them the keeper of the courts, sent to me to avert punishment. You remember you said, 'Here is the key. You may take away all the books in my stall, and all the MSS. on the stone slab. But please do not let the police take away my oil and wheat.' And I said to you, 'Do you not know that every house in which Bibles are found must be pulled down?' You said then, 'What shall we do?' I said, 'Get one of your people to take the Bibles into the yard that you use for your talks, and put them there, and I will come with the police to take them away.'

On further inquiry it turned out that the latter part of this letter was the forgery of a man called Ingentius, one of the secretaries of the court. But the picture it gives of the shifts in which magistrates and Christians too often took refuge is in the main correct.

Some of the Christians were made of sterner stuff. Of such was Felix, bishop of Tibjuca, a village near Carthage. The mayor of the town (*curator*) wrote to him 'to surrender his Scriptures, or some parchments of some sort', for the more merciful judges were often willing to take any 'waste scraps'. Felix refused. 'It is better,' he said, 'that I should be burnt myself rather than the Scriptures.' So he was hurried off to Carthage. 'Why don't you surrender some spare or useless books?' asked the proconsul Anulinus. But all subterfuges and hints were in vain. So, after a month of misery, Felix, heavily chained, was shipped off to Italy in the hold of a ship carrying horses, and at Venusia, in Apulia, with 'pious obstinacy', laid down his life rather than give up his Gospels.

Hermes, a deacon of Heraclea, in Thrace, who had at one time been its chief magistrate, was even more daring in his confidence:—

If we were to surender to you, torturer! all the Scriptures, so that there should be no trace left anywhere of this our true tradition, then our descendants will compose greater Scriptures, and will teach yet more earnestly the fear we have of Christ.

'Where did these come from?' asked Calvisianus, the Governor of Catania, in Sicily, of a Christian deacon called Euplius, who was discovered with a manuscript of the Gospels; 'did you bring them from your home?' 'I have no home, as my Lord Jesus Christ knows,' replied Euplius. 'Read them,' said the judge. So Euplius opened the books and read: 'Blessed are they which are persecuted for righteousness' sake, for theirs is the kingdom of heaven.' He turned over a few pages, and read again: 'Whosoever will come after Me, let him take up his cross and follow Me.' After many tortures Euplius was executed, repeating to the end, 'Thanks be to Christ my God.'

In the autumn of 304 the health of Diocletian failed. For forty years he had borne the burden of erecting a new empire out of chaos; now his mind refused to rise to higher themes than the opening of a new circus at Nicomedeia. Galerius and Maximian could thus pursue with less restraint their own designs. 'O Augustus,' shouted the mob to Maximian, on the occasion of a rare visit to Rome, 'no Christianity!' The cry fell in with Maximian's wishes. A fourth edict was issued affixing to Christianity the penalty of death, while the magistrates were informed that the entire population must be tested by sacrifices. Nobly did the Church respond to the call. The design of the pagans was more than met by the 'obstinacy' of the Christians. Hell was let loose in its vilest and most cruel forms; but against the onward march of the hosts of God its gates could not prevail.

The retirement of Diocletian (1 May 305) removed from the persecutors all restraint. Diocles, for the ex-emperor resumed his original name, settled down to cultivate his cabbages at Salona, in Dalmatia; Galerius and Maximin Daza – this last 'a young half savage, more accustomed to herds and woods', a kinsman of Galerius – addressed themselves to their task of crushing out the Church, though distracted for a while by many difficulties with regard to the succession. But the pace was too great to last, and in 308 mutilation was substitued for death as the punishment of the faith. At Caesarea Eusebius saw one day ninety-seven Christians, men, women, and even young children, on their way to the mines at Phaeno, each one minus the right eye, and with the left foot disabled by hot irons. For a few months the 'flame of persecution relaxed its violence, almost extinguished by the streams of sacred blood'. But in the autumn of 308 there began a new reign of terror, in the various acts of which we may trace the diabolical genius of Theotecnus, a Neoplatonist. A fifth edict appeared even more stringent than the previous. The fallen idols were to be re-erected, all households were to sacrifice, and, lest there should be any escape, all goods for sale in the markets were to be polluted by libations. For two years it rained blood. In some towns the streets were strewn with fragments of corpses. But in 311 Galerius relented. He was on his deathbed, tormented with the disease vulgarly known as the being eaten of worms. Like all the men of his day, he was the prey of superstition.

The gods whom he had defended had not helped him; perhaps it was not too late to appeal to the new deity. So from his dying bed he issued (30 April 311) his famous edict of toleration – 'ut denuo sint Christiani' – which bore also the signatures of Constantine and Licinius, or, as he should rightly be called after his elevation, Licinian, for Maxentius, who ruled in Italy, the son of Diocletian's colleague Maximian Herculius, was not recognized by the others as a lawful emperor. In this extraordinary document, wrung from a man by the terrors of the unknown, Galerius tried to dupe the Christians and their God into remitting for him the punishment of his cruelties. He had only persecuted, he maintained, to 'bring back to a good disposition the Christians who had abandoned the persuasion (*sectam*) of their own fathers' and 'the institutions of the ancients'. He confessed that he had failed to induce his victims 'to display due reverence for the gods, or pay heed to the God of the Christians'. So the edicts are rescinded; in return the Christians were expected 'to pray to their God for our recovery'. But it was too late. 'The unknown God to whom Galerius had at last betaken himself gave no answer to his insolent and tardy invocation.' Five days or so after the decree was posted at Nicomedeia Galerius died in Sardica. His dominions were shared between Maximin Daza and Licinian.

Maximin Daza had refused to affix his seal to his edict of toleration. He seems, however, to have issued some instructions of his own to the magistrates of the Eastern provinces, informing them that they 'need not for the present exert themselves further in the cause'. From a thousand prisons and *ergastula*, from mines and islands, the scarred warriors of Christ streamed home. Everywhere men began to re-erect their ruined churches, or to build new oratories over the graves of the sainted martyrs. But Theotecnus and his band did not intend thus tamely to yield. As Maximin toured round the East he was met by deputations from the heathen cities, urging that they might have local option in the matter of persecution. In Nicomedeia, to take one illustration recorded for us by Maximin himself, a huge memorial was presented to him, with due procession of gods and the like, asking permission to banish the atheists. At Tyre the town council put up a brass tablet forbidding Christianity within the city. On receiving the news, Maximin wrote to them his delight:

At last weakness has become strong. The night of error is scattering. The mist is breaking. . . . Ask what you like; you shall assuredly receive it.

At the same time steps were taken for the reformation of paganism. The Christian sacraments and institutions were imitated, a heathen hierarchy established of men of high rank. For the mob there was a clever winking Jove, for the devout a daily heathen service. To the new pontiffs was given the power of mulcting in noses, eyes, and ears those who absented themselves from the temples. Four prostitutes of Damascus professed that they had once been Christians, and had learned their trade by participating at Christian sacraments. Copies of their statements were circulated broadcast, while Theotecnus ordered that the infamous *Acts of Pilate*, which bespattered the Saviour with mud and His Cross with contempt, should be taught in all the schools.

The device of local option in persecution succeeded admirably. Wherever in the East the heathen were in a majority, they tried to cut down the leaders of the Church. Lucian of Antioch, Peter of Alexandria, Anthimus of Nicomedeia, are but three names out of a 'perfect choir of martyrs' who suffered at this time. Christian Armenia determined to interfere. The war which followed – the first crusade known to history – ended in the defeat of Daza.

At this stage a greater than Armenia intervened. The fortunes of Constantine, whose grandfather, on his mother Helena's side, kept a village inn in Dacia, from his birth to his famous ride from Nicomedeia across Europe back to his father Constantius' court at Boulogne, may be read elsewhere. The death of Constantius at York (25 July 306) was followed by his own elevation to the purple, with the title of Caesar. His passage of the Alps and subsequent victory over the vicious Maxentius at the Milvian Bridge (27 October 312) will stand out for ever in the annals of both Empire and Church. Constantine had seen his vision; henceforth he did homage to the conquering power of the Cross. The God of the Christians was too powerful to be despised. Pagan and Christian alike attributed his success to divine interposition – 'instinctu divinitatis', as the ambiguous inscription on his arch phrases it. With this conviction deeply implanted – we may call it Constantine's conversion provided we clearly understand our terms – the great statesman went down to Milan to meet his colleague Licinian. Thence he issued (March, 313) the famous document which marks an era in the history of the world.

'We have long seen', ran the edict, 'that we have no business to refuse freedom of religion. The power of seeing to matters of belief must be left to the judgement and desire of each individual, according to the man's own free will.'

The defeat of Daza by Licinian near Adrianople (30 April 313) turned the edict into accomplished fact in the East as well as the West. On 13 June 313 Lactantius heard the edict read aloud to the remnant of the sorely tried Church at Nicomedeia. A few weeks later Daza, a hunted fugitive, died of delirium tremens in Tarsus. Before the end came he had signified his adhesion to the policy of Constantine. He was the last of the persecutors to die. Diocletian, broken with disappointment and sickness, had already starved himself to death. He had seen the Church which he had tried to crush arise from the contest with still greater strength. The Empire was defeated; the Galilean had conquered. A new chapter had begun in the long annals of humanity.

Chapter Five

THE EXPERIENCES OF THE PERSECUTED

I

THE student should realize all that the profession of the Name involved. The persecution of Nero, that baptism of blood of the Roman Church, has been described for us by a master of language, the vividness of whose picture loses nothing from his manifest contempt for the Christians themselves struggling with his horror at the outrage, or his hatred of the tyrant. In a short chapter of Tacitus we have one of the most awful scenes of infamy of all time:

Mockery of every sort was added to their deaths. Covered with the skins of beasts, they were torn by dogs and perished, or were nailed to crosses, or were doomed to the flames and burnt, to serve as a nightly illumination when daylight had expired. Nero offered his gardens for the spectacle, and was exhibiting a show in the circus, while he mingled with the people in the dress of a charioteer or stood aloft in a car (*Ann.* xv 44).

We can see it all after the lapse of centuries, so lurid are the colours: the twofold entertainment, by night in the gardens thronged with Nero's guests, the victims in their pitchy tunics serving as living torches, while Nero drives round to gloat upon their agony; by day in the great wooden theatre of Caius the new sport, the hunt of men clad in the skins of wild beasts; the insults worse than death inflicted upon women and girls; and looking down upon all the selfsame obelisk from Heliopolis which has witnessed alike the oppression and deliverance of Israel in Egypt; the crucifixion of St. Peter, and the building of his famous church; the deaths of the martyrs and the fall of the Empire. Henceforth the Christians were known in the slang of the day as the *sarmenticii* or the *semaxii*, 'because bound to a half-axle stake we are burned in a circle of faggots'.

The Christian was ever exposed to a double danger; on the one hand popular hatred, on the other the wilfulness of the local magistrates, who could twist into an instrument of cruelty the very laws and procedure which had been devised to prevent injustice. For instance, the threefold chance of abjuring their religion before condemnation, which, as we see from Pliny's letter, was a right of the Christians, soon became a threefold torture to secure denial. For many governors there was no easier way of winning popularity with the mob than by the persecution of the Christians. Spies abounded, and the *delatores*, or professional accusers, were not slow in attempting to wring money from the Christians by the threat of reporting their crime. Add to this 'the threats and extortions of the soldiers and of private enemies'. In case of refusal, 'vile informers' entered the houses of the Christians 'by day and night and gave them up to pillage'. Murder, theft, gross crimes, 'tampering with family relations', were some of the charges, as we have already seen, that were freely brought against the Christians and accepted as proved by evidence wrung out from their servants by torture. Against them, as Seneca said of slaves, everything was lawful. City mobs laughed at the vile placards which caricatured their God, 'born of an ass, with the ears of an ass, hoofed in one foot, carrying a book and wearing a toga'; or drew an obscene representation of a cock with the inscription beneath, 'The Saviour of the world'. For the conscientious a new difficulty was added to life by the sprinkling of everything sold in the markets with heathen drink-offerings.

In the theatres mimes clothed in white garments parodied the Christian's hopes and sacred rites to the huge amusement of the crowd. But in one case the jest turned out to the furtherance of the Gospel. To please Diocletian, who happened to be present, the mime Genesius—

made sport of the Christian mysteries. 'I feel so heavy,' he cried, as he lay down on the stage as if he were ill, 'I want to be made light.' 'How are we to do it?' his companions cried. 'Are we to plane you as if we were carpenters?' 'Idiots,' replied Genesius; 'I want to die a Christian, that on that day I may fly up to God as refuge.' So they summoned a (sham) presbyter and exorcist. 'Why have you sent for us, my son?' they asked.

The rest of the story is one of the miracles of grace. Genesius, it would appear, had sprung from a Christian home in Arles; he had picked up his knowledge of religious phrases when a little lad. Of the story of his fall we know nothing, or rather we know all from ten thousand similar experiences. But now 'in a moment' the work of conviction began, and on the boards of the theatre, with mock priest and exorcist at his side, the laughing crowd all round, Genesius cried out, 'no longer in acting, but from an unfeigned desire: "I want to receive the grace of Christ, that I may be born again, and be set free from the sins which have been my ruin." ' The pantomime was turned into reality. The mock baptism over – for the crowd still thought he was acting – Genesius boldly proclaimed aloud his faith: 'Illustrious emperor, and all you people who have laughed loudly at this parody, believe me: Christ is the true Lord.' When Diocletian understood how matters lay he ordered Genesius to be stretched on the hobby-horse. His sides were torn with the claws, and burned with torches. But he kept repeating—

There is no king except Christ, whom I have seen and worship. For Him I will die a thousand times. I am sorry for my sin, and for becoming so late a soldier of the true King.

At length, as all tortures failed, Plautian the prefect ordered him to be beheaded.

When the storm broke, no retreat however secluded could save the persecuted from the pursuer; no station in life however humble was too lowly or insignificant to supply its victims:

> Remember what a martyr said
> On the rude tablet overhead!
> 'I was born sickly, poor, and mean,
> A slave: no misery could screen
> The holders of the pearl of price
> From Caesar's envy: therefore twice
> I fought with beasts, and three times saw
> My children suffer by his law.'

For the believer the routine of life itself became a martyrdom. 'We are banished,' wrote the Christians of Lyons, 'from the baths and forum; we are forbidden to appear in any public place whatever,' a boycott by no means unusual. The Christian lived at the mercy of the mob; who, stirred up by pagan priest or Jewish gold, might burst at any moment into his house and drag him forth to torture and death. 'Every one,' writes Phileas of Thmuis, 'had the liberty to abuse us as they pleased, with clubs, rods, and scourges.' 'We saw the mob' – we quote Dionysius of Alexandria in his description of the persecution of Decius—

suddenly burst into our dwellings as if by one common impulse. Every man entered some house known to him and began to spoil and destroy. All valuables were seized; things not worth carrying away, wooden funiture for instance, were burnt in the road. The scene resembled a town taken by storm.

When brought before the judge, the mob followed and clamoured for the Christian's condemnation. At other times, as in the case of Apollonia, in the same persecution at Alexandria, they took the law into their own hands, 'breaking all her teeth, and kindling a fire in which they threatened to burn her alive.' Even after death – though, to the honour of the Romans, this was rare – popular hatred pursued the Christians still, tearing their corpses from the tombs and cutting them in pieces, throwing to the dogs those who had died in prison 'that none should receive burial from us', or casting the ashes into the river, lest, as the cruel Maximus sneered, 'they should be tended by silly women and anointed with spices.'

Happy indeed were those Christians for whom kindly death soon ended all. Others were thrown into horrible prisons into which light and air could scarcely enter. In the persecution of Diocletian, 'dungeons destined for murderers and the vilest criminals were filled with bishops, presbyters, deacons, readers, exorcists, so that there was no room left for real criminals.' 'We have been cast,' write the martyrs of Carthage—

into two dungeons. There, doomed to die of hunger and thirst, our life is being consumed away. The stifling heat, caused by our crowded numbers, is intolerable. Eight days have passed since this letter was begun. During the last five days only bread and water have been doled out to us.

'You conquer hunger,' wrote Cyprian, 'despise thirst, and tread underfoot the squalor of the dungeon and its horrors by the vigour of your courage.' 'Prison,' exclaims Tertullian in his impassioned address *To the Martyrs (c. 2)*—

does the same service for the Christian which the desert did for the prophet. . . . Let us therefore drop the name of prison and call it a place of retirement. Though the body is shut in, all things are open to the spirit. In spirit, then, roam abroad, not setting before you shady paths or long colonnades but the way which leads to God. . . . The leg does not feel the chain if the mind is in heaven.

But even the horrors of the prison could not quench their faith and zeal. At Smyrna Pionius and his comrades, when flung into the darkest hole, 'sang without ceasing, Glory to Thee, O God.'

The one relief of the imprisoned Christians lay in the visits and charity of their brethren. These visits were allowed, possibly as the easiest way whereby the authorities could learn the names of others of the faith still at large, more probably because of the itching palms of the gaolers, and the indifference of the governors. So easy in fact was it to obtain admission that Cyprian found it necessary to urge the Christians of Carthage not to visit the prison in crowds, 'lest the means of access be denied.' But in the case of distinguished confessors, converse with whom was held to be itself a blessing, it was difficult to keep the Christians away from their cells. 'Creeping into gaol to kiss the martyrs' chains' was one of the things which the heathen husband, in the complaint of Tertullian, would not allow his Christian wife to do.

The prison system, by flinging the burden of support upon the prisoner, as was the case in all countries until recent days, lent itself to these visits. Lucian tells us that when Peregrinus, at that time a professor, was cast into prison, the Christians, especially the widows, 'looked after his wants with unremitting care and zeal, waiting about the doors of his gaol', sending in 'costly meals', and collecting large sums in Asia for his defence. We have a confirmation of this in the *Acts* of many martyrs, in the positive direction of the *Apostolic Constitutions*, as well as in the statement of Tertullian, that 'the monthly collection' – the law, as we have seen, would not allow collections more frequently – was spent, among other objects of charity, on the Christians banished to the islands and mines, 'so long as their distress is for the sake of God's fellowship.' This last clause was a needful precaution against designing rogues of the Peregrinus order, who tried to make out that their imprisonment for other misdemeanours was really on behalf on the faith, and thus sponged on the unfailing charity of the Church. Of the young Origen we are told that 'not only was he at the side of the holy martyrs in their imprisonment and until their final condemnation; when led out to death he boldly accompanied them'. Such ministries of love were not always without danger. In February, 309 or 310, five Egyptian travellers arrived before the gates of Caesarea. They were Christians who had accompanied their brethren to the mines in Cilicia, to act as good Samaritans, and who were now returning home. They were seized, and after incredible tortures entered 'the mighty portals of eternal life'. There were times when to give the kiss of brotherhood to one of the martyrs was itself to court instant death.

Of mob rule and its dangers to the Church no better illustration can be found than in the famous case of the Christians of Lyons. The persecution in that great capital of Gaul had begun in a boycott, rendered the more easy by the foreign origin – in part Greek, to some extent Phrygian – of the little Church. From this it passed to

hootings and blows, draggings, plunderings, starvings, and confinements, everything that an infuriated mob is wont to perpetuate against those whom they deem bitter enemies. And at length, being brought to the forum by the tribune of the soldiers, and the magistrates that had charge of the city, they were examined in the presence of the whole multitude; and having confessed they were shut up in prison until the arrival of the governor.

When the Christians were brought before the judgement seat, Vettius Epagathus, no alien but a young nobleman of Lyons,

asked that he should be heard in defence of his brethren. On this those who were round the judgement-seat so cried out against him that the governor, not for a moment listening to his just request, merely asked if he were a

Christian. And on his confessing in the clearest voice that he was, he was immediately taken up into the number of the martyrs.

When the aged bishop of Pothinus was brought to the bar, the mob

maltreated him in every way with their hands and feet, while those at a distance hurled at him whatever came to hand, for so they thought they would avenge their gods.

Before the persecution ceased forty-eight martyrs had won their discharge.

Or let the reader study the records of the presbyter Pionius, who was arrested with his companions 'on the birthday of the blessed martyr Polycarp.' See the little band on the eastern side of the square of Smyrna, surrounded by a brutal and jeering mob. They are not all 'of the Catholic Church.' One of the prisoners, Eutychian by name, is a Montanist; another, Metrodore, is 'a presbyter of the Marcionites'; yet they are one in the courage and loyalty of their faith. A slave girl, Sabina, in her terror at the threats of a punishment worse than death, was clinging to Pionius. 'Look,' cried a wit, 'the babe is afraid she is going to be robbed of her mother's milk.' Others handled the ropes, and asked ironically: 'And what are these for?' Said the contractor for the public games to the martyr Asclepiades, 'I am going to ask for you to fight in my son's exhibition of gladiators'; while a police officer gave Pionius a knock on the head so violent that the blood ran. All this was but preliminary to the clawings and burnings with which the festival concluded.

Apart altogether from mob rule, the Christian was at all times exposed to dangers, not the less formidable because legal. We have an illustration of these dangers in the case of Julitta, a wealthy widow of Caesarea, in Cappadocia, who brought an action to recover some property of which she had been wrongfully dispossessed. The rogue pleaded that the widow was a Christian, and therefore not entitled to seek legal redress. The case actually ended in the burning of Julitta. Truly might it have been said of the early believers: 'In the midst of life we are in death.'

II

What shall we say of the punishments and of the tortures which formed part of the judicial processes by which evidence was sought to be extracted from the Christians? Roman citizens as a rule were sent to the capital; for them there was the long misery of the journey in company with brutal guards. Finally, as an act of special 'benevolence', they were handed over, as St. Paul, to the headsman; though the law in this matter was not strictly observed. Inasmuch as they were often charged with *majestas*, their citizenship did not always save them from the tortures, endless in the variety and ingenuity of their cruelty, which for non-citizens were almost inevitable.

In the later martyrologies there is a manifest tendency to pile up the horrors. But if we confine ourselves to strictly historical cases, the savagery, though to a large extent a part of the ordinary judicial processes of the age, is appalling. Some, suffering the punishment of parricides, were shut up in a sack with snakes and thrown into the sea; others were tied to huge stones and cast into a river. For Christians the cross itself was not deemed sufficient agony; hanging on the tree, they were beaten with rods until their bowels gushed out, while vinegar and salt were rubbed into their wounds. In the Thebais, during the persecution of Diocletian, Christians were tied to catapults, and so wrenched limb from limb. Some, like Ignatius, were thrown to the beasts; others tied to their horns. Women were stripped, enclosed in nets, and exposed to the attacks of furious bulls. Many were 'made to lie on sharp shells', and tortured with scrapers, claws, and pincers, before being delivered to the mercy of the flames. Not a few were broken on the wheel, or torn in pieces by wild horses. Of some the feet were slowly burned away, cold water being poured over them the while lest the victims should expire too rapidly. Peter, one of the servants of Diocletian, was scourged to the bone, then placed near a grid-iron that he might witness the roasting of pieces torn from his own body. At Lyons they tried to overcome the obstinacy of Sanctus of Vienne 'by fixing red-hot plates of brass to the most delicate parts of his body'. After this he was slowly roasted in the iron chair. Down the backs of others 'melted lead, hissing and bubbling, was poured'; while a few, 'by the clemency of the emperor', escaped with the searing out of their eyes, or the tearing off of their legs. These instances – but a few out of a long catalogue that might be compiled – will show what it cost to witness the good confession; to say nothing of the rack, the hobby-horse, the claws, and other tortures preparatory to the sentence.

Fortunate were those for whom there was the relief of death. Some were banished to the mines of 'deadly Sardinia', and there, with fetters on their limbs, insufficient food, almost naked, beaten with clubs by savage overseers, passed a life of ceaseless toil amid surroundings of indescribable filth. Others were denied even the refuge of the mines, and were dragged about from town to town in the train of the governor, and exhibited for the sport of the people.

For women there were punishments worse than death, the least of which was their exposure almost naked in the arena. Perpetua was not alone in the horror she felt when she dreamed that 'she was stripped, turned into the arena, and rubbed down with oil as they do for the games.' In the great persecution under Diocletian in the Thebais, if we may trust Eusebius, women were tied to trees by one foot and there left to perish, hanging downwards, stark naked. They were more fortunate than some of their sisters, many of whom were dragged to the brothels to suffer shame before being led to the stake or cast to the lions. 'Either sacrifice to the gods or be handed over to infamy' was the awful dilemma which confronted more than one Christian maiden. The danger was real, for the Roman mob had twisted a regulation, originally framed in the interests of humanity, into the occasion of bestial cruelty. 'Christians to the panthers, virgins to the pandars,' was no mere jest, but part of the cost that must be paid 'for Christ's sake'. In the romances of the early mediaeval Church the chastity of these maidens is always miraculously preserved amidst the most unholy surroundings; but probably the actual facts were often otherwise. They paid a price dearer than life rather than deny their Lord. Said Theodora of Alexandria when the judge read to her the brutal order: 'If you force me to do this, I do not think that God will count it a sin.' Some sought escape in the destruction of their beauty, or even in suicide. Potamiaena of Alexandria, whose beauty was noted, was told that unless she recanted she should be given over to the lust of gladiators. She escaped by a defiance so daring that the judge in his anger 'ordered boiling pitch to be poured over her limbs, gradually working up from the feet to the crown of the head.' For three hours she suffered agonies, until the pitch reached her neck.' Such horrors, no doubt, were exceptional, and limited to the frenzied East. But the untold heroism of women, not a few, should not altogether be forgotten in these latter days.

III

The question is sometimes asked, not merely from motives of curiosity: What was the experience of the martyr as he thus passed through his great renunciation? The materials for answering the question are abundant, and the answer has a spiritual value of its own. We believe it can be shown that Christ alone really suffered all the horror of His martyrdom—

Yea, once Immanuel's orphaned cry His universe hath shaken,
It went up single, echoless, 'My God, I am forsaken.'

Thus Christ alone *tasted* death, drained the cup of its bitters to the dregs. For others there was a grace of God which dulled the pain, turning agony into victory. When the great day came, and they passed into the furnace, lo! there was One standing beside them, like unto the Son of Man, and so 'they found the fire of their inhuman torturers cold.'

We believe that Browning is right when in his Epitaph in the Catacombs he lays stress upon the absence of all remembrance of time in the sufferer. But remembrance of time is the measure of the consciousness of pain:

> I was some time in being burned,
> But at the close a Hand came through
> The fire above my head, and drew
> My soul to Christ, whom now I see.
> Sergius, a brother, writes for me
> This testimony on the wall –
> For me, I have forgot it all.

When Mr. Fearing came to the river, Bunyan saw that the waters were so low that he passed over almost dryshod. The early Church was not without its Mr. Fearing, and Mr. Despondency's daughter Much-Afraid; timid souls, who dreaded that when the trial came they would be found wanting. But when they passed through the dark valley He was there, and their fear left them. 'Sufferings borne for the Name are not torments,' said the martyr Maximus of Ephesus, as they stretched him on the hobby-horse, 'but soothing ointments.' 'O blessed martyrs,' cries Tertullian,

you have gone out of prison, rather than into one. . . . Your dungeon is full of darkness, but ye yourselves are light; it has bonds, but God has made you free.

The absence of all fear, in fact, is one of the notes of the early Church. Cyprian was right when he speaks of 'the white-robed cohort of Christ's soldiers' as 'passing through footprints of glory to the embrace and kiss of Christ.' Theirs was a triumphal march along a greater Sacred Way than Roman conquerors ever trod. 'These are not chains,' exclaims Cyprian,

they are ornaments. O fettered feet of the blessed ones treading the path to Paradise! You have no bed, no place to rest in the mines; your wearied limbs are stretched on the cold earth; naked, there are no clothes to cover you; hungry, no bread to feed you. But what a glory lights up this your shame!

The cause was not far to seek; 'The Holy Ghost has entered the prison with you', the Lord Jesus was suffering in them and with them; and so a secret spell preserved them in their living death.

No tale of early centuries is more familiar than the story of the passion of Polycarp – the most ancient example known of 'Acts of Martyrdom'. On his way to his own passion in Rome Ignatius had exhorted the young bishop, of whose early life we know little save his intimacy with St. John, 'to stand firm as an anvil when it is smitten. A great athlete should receive blows and conquer'. Nearly half a century later the 'athlete' received his crown, a few months only after his return from a journey which, in the interests of ecclesiastical unity, the old man had found it necessary to make to Rome.

The annual festival of Caesar was in progress at Smyrna. As was usually the case, the occasion was turned to profit by the enemies of Christ. Eleven martyrs, mostly from Philadelphia, had already fought with beasts. One of them, Germanicus by name, when exhorted by the proconsul 'to have pity on his youth,' dragged the beast to him that he might the quicker perish. The cry arose: 'Away with the Atheists; let search be made for Polycarp.' By the torture of a slave the aged bishop's hiding-place was found. Mounted police were despatched; late at night they burst into the upper room of a small cottage. 'God's will be done,' said Polycarp, and requested a short time for prayer. This was granted; the police were busy at the supper which the saint provided for them, and in nowise anxious to journey back in the dark. For two hours he stood in intercession 'for the Catholic Church'; then as morning was breaking set off to the city, riding on an ass. The captain of the police, one Herod by name, together with his father Nicetes, met him on the way, and took him into their chariot, endeavouring to persuade him to recant and say: 'Caesar is Lord.' Their interest was not merely that of officials; perhaps Herod was thinking of the peril of his own sister Alce, one of Polycarp's flock. But all their efforts were vain; so, on Polycarp's repeated refusal, they thrust him out of the chariot with such violence that 'he bruised his shirt'. On his entrance into the arena, 'our people who were present heard a voice, though no man saw the speaker: 'Polycarp, be strong, and play the man.' 'Swear,' said the proconsul, 'by the genius of Caesar; retract and say, Away with the atheists.' The proconsul, Titus Statius Quadratus, mistaking Polycarp's meaning, pressed him further: 'Swear, and I release thee; blaspheme Christ.' 'Eighty and six years,' was the immortal reply, 'have I served Christ, and He has never done me wrong. How can I blaspheme my King, who saved me?' After further entreaties, the proconsul threatened to throw him to the beasts or burn him alive. ' 'Tis well,' replied Polycarp; 'I fear not the fire that burns for a season and after a while is quenched. Why delayest thou? Come, do what thou wilt.' So the herald thrice proclaimed, 'Polycarp has confessed himself a Christian.' A howl of vengeance rose from the heathen, in which the Jews, who were present in large numbers, joined – it was 'a great sabbath', probably the feast of Purim, and their fanaticism was specially excited. 'This,' they cried, 'is the teacher of Asia, the overthrower of our gods, who has perverted so many from sacrifice and adoration.' So they desired the Asiarch, one Gaius Julius Philippus of Trales, as inscriptions show, to let loose upon him a lion. The Asiarch excused himself; the games in honour of Caesar were over; he had exhausted his stock of beasts.

So the mob with one accord lifted up its voice, clamouring that he should be burnt alive. The execution followed close upon the sentence. The wood for the stake, torn in an instant from shops and baths, was carried to the fatal spot by eager hands, the Jews as usual freely offering their services.

The old man was stripped. But

As they were going to nail him to the stake: 'Leave me,' he said, 'as I am, for He that hath granted me to endure the fire will grant me also to endure the pile unmoved, even without the security that ye seek from the nails.' So they did not nail him, but tied him.

Then he offered his last prayer:

O Lord God Almighty, the Father of Thy well-beloved and ever-blessed Son, Jesus Christ, by whom we have received the knowledge of Thee, . . . I thank Thee that Thou hast graciously thought me worthy of this day and of this hour, that I may receive a portion among the number of martyrs, in the cup of Thy Christ.

No sooner had he uttered his Amen, than the fire was kindled and blazed up. But it arose, curving like an arch or the bellying sail of a ship, leaving him in the centre like a treasure of gold or silver, unharmed. The student will remember the similar cases of Savonarola and Hooper of Gloucester. An executioner was sent to give the *coup de grâce*. To the amazement of the spectators, blood flowed in streams from the aged body and extinguished the flames. In their fear lest the body should fall into the hands of the Christians, the Jews took steps, using Nicetes as their leader, to have it thrust back into the midst of the fire. At the moment of Polycarp's death, his pupil Irenaeus, then on a visit to Rome, heard a voice as of a trumpet saying, 'Polycarp has been martyred.' By his death 'Polycarp stayed the persecution, having, as it were, set his seal upon it.' The annual festival of Caesar was over, and the excited mob returned to their homes.

'The martyrdom of Cyprian,' writes Gibbon, 'will convey the clearest information of the spirit and of the forms of Roman persecution.' We may add that few of the *Acts* keep more close to the original official records. During the severe persecution of Decius, Cyprian, at that time undoubtedly the most distinguished prelate of Western Christendom, had yielded to counsels of prudence and withdrawn for a while from Carthage (Jan. 250). In the spring of 251 he had returned, and had distingued himself by the zeal with which he had flung himself into the work of visiting the plague-stricken city (A.D. 252). Under his lead, Christians 'just emerged from the mines or the prison, with the scars or the mutilations of recent tortures upon their bodies, were soon exposing their limbs, if possible, to a more honourable martyrdom.' But such works of charity did not lessen the hostility of the heathen, who looked upon the plague as the chastisement of the gods for their toleration of an unnatural religion. On the renewal of the persecution by Valerian (257), Cyprian, who did not this time withdraw from the city, was summoned before the proconsul Paternus, and ordered to return to the practice of the religion of his ancestors (30 Aug 257). On his refusal he was banished to Curubis, fifty miles from Carthage, though after a while he was suffered to return to his former country house. Shortly after the accession of a new proconsul, Galerius Maximus, Cyprian was once more apprehended, and brought to Carthage. He was lodged for the night in the private house of one of his gaolers, and treated with respect and consideration. All through the night the streets were filled with a vast but orderly crowd of enemies and friends. In the morning Cyprian, whose habitual seriousness of countenance was transfigured with joyfulness, was brought before the proconsul. No words were wasted. 'Art thou,' said the judge, 'Thascius Cyprian, the bishop (*papa*) of many impious men? The most sacred emperors command thee to sacrifice.' 'I will not,' replied the bishop. 'Consider well,' was the answer. 'Execute your orders,' replied Cyprian; 'the case admits of no consideration.' With some reluctance the judge, after conferring with his council read the sentence:

That Thascius Cyprian should be immediately beheaded, as the enemy of the gods of Rome and, as the standard-bearer and ring-leader of a criminal association which he had seduced into an impious resistance against the laws of the most holy emperors, Valerian and Gallienus (Geb. AMS 127).

'God be thanked,' answered the bishop, when the reading on the sentence was finished. 'We will die with him,' shouted the Christians; but Cyprian was led away under an escort of the famous Third Legion to a plain near the city, or rather a natural amphitheatre with steep, high slopes, thick with trees, into which the spectators climbed. There his presbyters and deacons were allowed to assist him in laying aside his garments. With his usual indifference to money, the bishop desired his friends to hand the executioner twenty-five gold pieces, a fee of about

£15. Meanwhile his friends strewed the ground with handkerchiefs, with a view to future relics and momentoes. This done, Cyprian covered his face with a cloth; the sword of the executioner flashed, and at one blow the head was severed from the body (14 Sept 258).

Of all the stories of martyrdom in early times none is more unexaggerated, true to life and human nature, than the story of the two Carthaginian martyrs, Perpetua and Felicitas, who appear to have suffered on the birthday of Geta, the worthless son of Septimius Severus. Vibia Perpetua – one of the few saints still honoured in the Anglican calendar – with her ecstatic visions and her unconquerable faith, is in very deed one of the heroic figures of the early Church. Of good family, liberal education, and honourably married, Perpetua tells her own story, though the introduction and completion are by another hand, possibly Tertullian's. She was but twenty-two when arrested and cast into prison:

I was terrified; never before had I experienced such awful darkness. O dreadful day! the heat overpowering by reason of the crowd of prisoners, the extortions of the guard. Above all, I was torn with anxiety for my babe.

Two deacons, Tertius and Pomponius, obtained her removal for some hours a day to a better room:

There I sat suckling my babe, who was slowly wasting away. Nevertheless the prison was made to me a palace, where I would rather have been than anywhere else.

In part her joy was due to her visions. In one of these Perpetua saw a ladder of gold, the top of which rested in heaven. Beyond the highest rung, surrounded by a white-robed throng, stood the Good Shepherd in the midst of a wonderful garden like unto Eden. But on either side of the ladder were instruments of torture, while a terrible dragon guarded the approach. Up this ladder of gold, so narrow that only one could climb at a time, the saints passed to God. But they must first crush the dragon's head ere they could hear the welcome of the Shepherd: 'Thou hast borne thee well, child.' For Perpetua the 'crushing' was without hesitation. When brought before the judge, she was ordered to sacrifice to the emperor. She refused, and was condemned with her comrades to fight the beasts. 'So we went with joy to our prison.'

We must not forget Felicitas. When arrested with Perpetua, she was in the eighth month of pregnancy. As the day of the games approached she feared above all lest on that account her martyrdom should be postponed. So her 'brother martyrs prayed with united groaning', and her travail began.

As she lay in her agony in the crowded gaol the keeper of the stocks said to her, 'If you cannot endure these pains, what will you do when you are thrown to the beasts?' 'I suffer now alone,' she replied, 'but then there will be One in me who will suffer for me because I shall suffer for Him.'

Perpetua maintained her calmness to the end. When a tribune, who had the popular idea that the Christians dealt in the black art, and so might escape from prison by their enchantments, dealt harshly with the prisoners, she reminded him that since they were to fight on Caesar's birthday they ought not to disgrace Caesar by their condition. On their last night they joined together in the agapé. The lovefeast was interrupted by people whose curiosity had led them to visit the prison, that they might see what sort of victims would be provided on the morrow. 'Mark well our faces,' said Saturus, 'that you may recognize us again on the day of judgement.'

When the day of victory dawned, the Christians marched in procession from the prison to the arena as if they were marching to heaven, with joyous countenances, agitated rather by gladness than fear. Perpetua followed, with radiant step, as became the bride of Christ, the dear one of God.

Attempts were made to force them to put on certain dresses, the men the robes of those devoted to Saturn, the women of Ceres. They refused, and 'injustice recognized the justice' of their refusal. So they marched to death in their own garments, 'Perpetua singing Psalms, for she was now treading down the Egyptian's head.' In the arena Saturus was exposed on a slightly raised platform to the attack of a bear. As the beast would not leave its den, he was handed over to a leopard, who with one bite covered him with blood. The mob called out in their glee, in derision of the Christian rite of baptism, 'That's the bath that brings salvation.' The two women, one of them scarce recovered from childbirth, were hung up in nets, lightly clad, to be gored by a bull. When Perpetua was tossed her first thought was of her shame, as she tried to cover herself with her torn tunic. 'She then clasped up her hair, for it did not become a martyr to suffer with dishevelled locks, lest she should seem to be mourning in her glory.' This done she raised up Felicitas, and 'the cruelty of people being for a while appeased,' they were permitted to retire. Perpetua herself seemed in a trance. 'When are we to be tossed?' she asked, and could scarcely be induced to believe that she had suffered, in spite of the marks on her body. Finally the two heroines of God were put to death by gladiators. After exhorting the others 'to stand fast in the faith and love one another,' Perpetua, 'first stabbed between the bones that she might have the more pain, guided to her own throat the uncertain hand of the young gladiator.' So she too passed over, and all the trumpets sounded for her on the other side.

IV

Not the least part of the agony of Perpetua, as well as of other martyrs, lay in the frenzied entreaties of loved ones, oftentimes brought by the magistrates into the hall of justice for the very purpose. Origen was right: 'It is the love of wife and children that fills up the measure of martyrdom.' For Perpetua there were the entreaties of her aged heathen father, the wailings of the babe at her breast:

When I was in the hands of the persecutors, my father in his tender solicitude tried hard to pervert me from the faith. 'My father,' I said, 'you see this pitcher; can we call it by any other name than what it is?' 'No,' he said, 'Nor can I call myself by any other name than that of Christian.' So he went away, but, on the rumour that we were to be tried, returned, wasted away with anxiety: 'Daughter,' he said, 'have pity on my grey hairs; have compassion on thy father. Do not give me over to disgrace. Behold thy brothers, thy mother, thy aunt; behold thy child who cannot live without thee. Do not destroy us all.' Thus spake my father, kissing my hands, and throwing himself at my feet. And I wept because of my father, for he alone of all my family would not rejoice in my martyrdom. So I comforted him, saying: 'In this trial what God determines will take place. We are not in our own keeping, but in God's.' So he left me weeping bitterly. (Robinson o.c. 62–4; Geb. AMS 64–6.)

But when the day of trial came her father was once more at the bar, calling out to the mother as he held her child in his arms, 'Have pity on your babe.'

When Phileas of Thmuis was brought before Culcian, the prefect of Egypt, the trusted friend of Maximin, Culcian tried with many arguments to induce him to sacrifice. 'Have you,' he asked, 'a conscientious objection?' On Phileas replying, 'Yes': 'Why does not conscience,' pursued the prefect, 'tell you to pay regard to the interests of your wife and children?' 'Because a conscience Godwards has a higher claim,' was the answer. Upon this the officials of the court, the mayor of Thmuis, together with his family, threw themselves at his feet, beseeching the bishop to have pity on his wife and children. But he stood 'like a rock unmoved' until 'his unquenchable spirit was set free by the sword'.

Over Irenaeus of Sirmium – a city on the Save near its union with the Danube – his children, wife, and parents lamented with bitter groans: 'have pity on yourself and us'; while his friends implored him to have pity on his tender youth. 'My Lord Jesus,' was the reply, 'told us that he that loved father or mother more than Me was not worthy of Me.' To Felicitas of Rome: 'Have pity,' said the judge, 'on your sons, young men in the prime of life.' 'Your exhortation,' replied Felicitas, 'is cruel mockery.' Then turning to her sons: 'Lads,' she said, 'look up and behold the heavens where Christ awaits you with His saints. Fight for your souls and show yourselves faithful in the love of Christ.' 'Dionysia of Alexandria, the mother of many children', we are told, 'did not love them more than the Lord', simple words which conceal the depths of anguish through which she passed. In the case of Afra of Augsburg, a converted prostitute, who is reputed to have suffered in the terror of Diocletian, we are introduced to a new form of temptation of even more subtle power

'I hear you were a prostitute,' said the judge; 'sacrifice, then, for the God of Christians will have nothing to do with you.' 'My Lord,' she replied, 'said that He came down from heaven to save sinners such as me.'

In spite of all reproaches and arguments, she persisted in her faith in the power of Christ to save even to the uttermost. So she too was handed over to the flames. Thus the harlot gained what Cyprian rightly calls 'the purple robe of the Lamb'.

For weeks before the fatal issue, we find the martyrs living in a state of ecstasy. They see the heavens open, and the triumphant ones that follow the Lamb riding upon white horses. Three days before his capture, Polycarp dreamed that his pillow was on fire, this he interpreted as signifying by what death he should glorify God. In most of the records we have visions of recent martyrs. On the night before her fight with the beasts Perpetua dreamed that the martyred deacon Pomponius came to her cell. 'Come,' he said, 'for we are waiting for thee.'

So he held my hand, and we began to climb by rough and winding ways. At length, gasping for breath, we came to the amphitheatre. There he placed me in the middle of the arena and said, 'Fear not, I am here with thee.'

In her dream she fought with a foul Egyptian gladiator, but one stood by 'with a green branch in his hand on which were apples of gold.' At last Perpetua threw the Egyptian down and received the bough. When she awoke, 'I knew,' she said, 'the victory was mine.' She had seen 'the devil rolling in the dust'.

Marianus, martyr possibly of Cirta, dreamed that he saw a great scaffold, on which the judge was condemning to the sword bands of Christians. 'My turn came. Then I heard a great voice saying, "Fasten Marianus up." ' So he too mounted the scaffold; but, lo, instead of the judge, he found himself amidst green fields and grass waving with sunlight, holding the hand of the martyr Cyprian, who smiled, as he said, 'Come and sit beside me.' The day before this dream Marianus had been hung up by the thumbs, with unequal weights tied to his feet, while his body had been torn by an iron claw. In the awful thirst which such torture brings, we can understand the further vision; how he saw

a dell in the midst of the woods, with a full clear spring flowing with many waters. Then Cyprian caught up a bowl which lay beside the spring, filled it and drained it, filled it again and reached it out to me, and I drank it, nothing loath. As I was saying, Thanks be to God, I woke at the sound of my own voice.

Saturus, the companion of Perpetua, had a vision in which he was carried by four angels into the midst of heaven itself, 'though their hands touched us not'. There, in a palace 'whose walls were built of light', and which stood in the midst of fields covered with violets and other flowers, he 'heard the voice of those who sing unceasingly, Holy, Holy, Holy,' and received the kiss of Christ:

There also we found Jecondus and Saturninus, and Artaxious who had been burnt alive in the same persecution, and Quintus who had died as a martyr in prison (Geb. AMS 80).

Quartillosia, who suffered in the same persecution as Marianus, whose husband and son had witnessed the good confession three days before, saw her son enter the prison in which she herself lay, expecting death.

And he sat on the brim of a fountain and said, 'God hath seen your tribulation and labour.' And after him entered a young man, wonderfully tall, carrying two bowls of milk in his hands. And from these bowls he gave us all to drink; and the bowls failed not. And suddenly the stone which divided the window in the middle was taken away, letting in the free face of the sky (Geb. AMS 149).

But the images in the martyrs' dreams are not always those of thirst, of green fields and orchards, or of the free breezes, natural as such dreams are to tortured souls in prison. Renus, another of the same band of African martyrs, had a vision in which he saw his companions brought into court one by one; 'as each one advanced, a lantern was carried before him'. When he awoke and told his story to his comrade in prison, 'then were we glad, having confidence to walk with Christ, who is a lantern to our feet.' A martyr named Flavian, one of Cyprian's flock at Carthage, dreamed that he asked his bishop 'whether the death-stroke was painful.' And Cyprian answered and said, 'The body does not feel when the mind is wholly devoted to God.' On the night before his martyrdom, another of the same devoted company, James of Cirta, dreamed that he saw the martyred bishop Agapius

surrounded by all the others who were imprisoned with us, holding a joyous feast. Marianus and I were carried away by the spirit of love to join it, as if to one of our love-feasts, when a boy ran to meet us, who turned out to be one of the twins who had suffered three days before in company with their mother. He had a wreath of roses round his neck, and bore a green palm in his right hand. And he said, 'Rejoice and be glad, for tomorrow you shall sup with us.'

In her first vision Perpetua saw the Good Shepherd, who gave her a morsel of cheese, which she ate with folded hands! When she awoke with the sweet taste in her mouth, 'we knew that our passion was at hand.'

Nor were the ecstasies limited to the martyrs themselves: the Christians who witnessed their sufferings also dreamed their dreams and saw their visions. We have an instance of this in the last chapter of the Antiochene *Acts of Martyrdom of St. Ignatius*, one of the few fragments true to life in an otherwise worthless romance. There the writer tells how

we weak men, after what had passed, when we fell asleep for a while, some of us suddenly beheld the blessed Ignatius standing by and embracing us, while by others again he was seen praying over us, and by others dripping with sweat, as if he were come from a hard struggle, and were standing at the Lord's side, with much boldness and unutterable glory (Lightf. *Ign.* ii 49).

After the burning of Fructuosus, the bishop of Tarragona, and his deacons (21 January 259), two of the Christian servants of the judge saw the martyrs ascending to heaven, 'with their chains still upon them, but crowns on their brows', and pointed them out to the governor's daughter. She fetched her father, 'who, however, was not worthy to see them'. But at Alexandria the vision of the martyr Potamiaena led to the conversion of many heathen who had witnessed her sufferings. To the same exalted and nervous condition we may well attribute the strange sweet smells, the heavenly voices, and other incidents which the faithful were quick to discern at the passing of their heroes. At Lyons the martyrs, we are told, 'were so fragrant with the sweet odour of Christ that some bystanders supposed that they had been anointed with myrrh'. At the execution of Polycarp, his friends heard a voice from heaven calling upon him to play the man; after his death there arose from his ashes, as they thought, a fragrant odour 'like the fumes of incense, or other fragrant drugs'.

When the day of their trial came, the confidence of the Christians – Pliny, in his famous letter, had called it their 'inflexible obstinacy' – was in no wise shaken. The Roman court, with its instruments of torture, set out in grim array – the hobby-horse, the claws, the rack, the heated irons, the boiling oil – the howling mob, the insignia of an imperial power, from which there was no escape, did not overawe the confessors.

Theirs was the confidence of the Angel of Repentance in the *Shepherd* of Hermas – one of the books that profoundly influenced the early martyrs, as we may learn from the allusions to it in the story of Perpetua—

Fear not the Devil, for there is no power in him against you. The Devil hath fear alone, but his fear hath no force. The Devil can wrestle against you, but wrestle you down he cannot!

In all churches the day of martyrdom became known as the confessor's 'birthday', a joyous term, significant of much. At the martyrdom of Polycarp, eleven heroes from Philadelphia

were so torn with lashes that the inward veins and arteries were visible, so that the very bystanders had pity and wept. But they themselves uttered neither cry nor groan, thus proving to us all that at that hour the martyrs of Christ, though tortured, were absent from the flesh, or rather, that the Lord was standing by and conversing with them (*Mart. Polyc.* 2).

When the Scillitan martyrs, seven men and five women, were condemned by Saturninus at Carthage: 'We give God thanks,' cried one; 'Today we shall be in heaven,' added a second. This talk of heaven sometimes bewildered, sometimes amused the magistrates. 'Do you suppose,' said the prefect Junius Rusticus to Justin and his companions, 'that you will ascend up to heaven to receive some recompense there?' 'I do not suppose,' was Justin's answer, 'for I know it, and am persuaded of it.' 'Earth,' cried Cyprian, in the same spirit of assurance,

is shut against us, but heaven is opened; death overtakes us, but immortality follows: the world recedes, but Paradise receives. What honour, what peace, what joy, to shut our eyes on the world and men, and open them on the face of God and His Christ! Oh, short and blessed voyage! (*de Exhort. Mart.* 13).

Of Dativus we read that he was 'rather a spectator of his own tortures than a sufferer.' When Carpus was nailed upon the cross he was observed to smile. 'What made you laugh?' asked his tormentors, in astonishment. 'I saw the glory of the Lord, and was glad,' was the answer. Standing by was a woman named Agathonice. She caught the infection of his enthusiasm. 'That dinner,' she cried, 'is prepared for me'; then tore off her garments and laid herself upon the cross. So great was the Christians' eagerness and confidence, that Saturninus – one of the friends of Perpetua – used to say to his companions in prison, as they talked over their coming fate, 'that he wished he could fight all the beasts, that so he might win a more glorious crown.' When Phileas of Thmuis was condemned to the sword: 'Present my thanks,' he said, 'to the emperors, for they have made me joint heir with Christ.' When the cruel Datian ordered his executioners to furrow the sides of the young girl Eulalia of Merida in Spain: 'Lord,' she cried, 'they are writing that Thou art mine.' At the trial of James of Cirta, the attention of the heathen in court was drawn to one of the bystanders. So joyous was his mien, that the magistrates, in suspicion, asked him if he were not a Christian – for, added the writer, 'Christ shone in his face and bearing.' Babylas of Antioch saw six of his catechumens perish before his eyes. He then laid his head upon the block, saying, 'Here am I, O God, and the children whom Thou hast given me.' According to Chrysostom, whose evidence in this particular may be trusted, his chains were buried with him, by his own desire, 'to show to the world that the things which the world despises are the glory of the Christian'.

Both Aristides and Celsus find fault with the Christians for their mixture of humility and arrogance. At the bar the assurance of the Christians was overwhelming. Oftentimes the confessor lectured his judge, as if they, not he, were pleading for their lives. 'You judge us, but God shall judge you,' said the Carthaginian martyrs – the friends of Perpetua – to the prefect Hilarian; nor were they daunted by the cries of the people, that for this insult they should be scourged. For the martyrs believed, in the words of Tertullian, that the day should come when they 'would judge their judges.' 'Sacrifice or die,' said the proconsul Marcian to Achatius, who seems to have been a bishop of one of the lesser Antiochs, or of some village near Antioch. 'That is what the highwaymen of Dalmatia say,' was the contemptuous reply, 'when they meet you in a dark, narrow lane. Your verdicts are of the same order.' Claudius, a young Christian of Aegea, in Cilicia, was placed on a hobby-horse and flames applied to his feet, while the claw tore his sides. 'Fool and madman,' cried the youth to his judge, 'do you not care for what the Lord will make you pay for this? You are blind, altogether blind!' Andronicus, another of the many martyrs of Cilicia, was beaten with raw hides until his whole body was one wound. 'Rub his back well with salt,' said the cruel Flavius Numerianus Maximus. 'You must rub in more salt than that,' was the joking answer, 'if I am to keep.' 'You cursed fellow,' said Maximus, 'you talk to me as if you were my equal.' 'I am not your equal,' retorted the Christian, 'but I have the right to talk.' 'I will cut out your right, you ruffian,' cried the judge. 'You will never be able to do that,' said the prisoner, 'neither you, nor your father Satan, nor the devils whom you serve.' 'Take hold of his cheeks and rip them up,' said Maximus, as another of the same band, Tarachus by name, stood before him for the third time of torture, with jaws crushed, ears burnt off, his body one mass of wounds. 'Don't think,' replied Tarachus, 'that you can terrify me with your words; I am ready for you at all points, for I wear the

armour of God!' A long dialogue followed, but all the varied tortures of
the judge were powerless to break the daring defiance and contempt of
the prisoner. Against such men the gates of hell could not prevail. 'These
are they,' said St. Cyprian, with a glance back at his heathen days—

whom we held sometimes derision, and as a proverb of reproach. We fools
counted their life madness, and their end to be without honour. How are
they numbered among the children of God, and their lot is among the
saints!

The Christian's contempt of death was remarkable even in an age in
which indifference to death formed one of the pleasures of life. The
satirist Lucian tells us, with laughter, of the contempt of death which
led the Christians, as well as the Cynics, with whom they were often
confounded, to surrender themselves of their own free will to martyrdom, and thus 'bring a golden life to a golden close'. 'These imbeciles,'
he sneered, 'are persuaded that they are absolutely immortal, and that
they will live for ever.' 'Our young men and maidens,' boasts Minucius
Felix, writing a few years later, 'mock your crosses and tortures, your
wild beasts and all the terrors of your punishments!' With this agrees
the testimony of Cyprian: 'The tortured stood more firm than the torturers; the torn limbs overcame the hooks that tore them.' 'The Christians,'
writes another, 'all disregard the world and despise death.' 'Christianus
sum' – the fatal confession to which there was but one issue – was the
sole answer to all their questions which the magistrates of Antioch could
extort from Lucian. 'Condemnation,' said Tertullian, 'gives us more
pleasure than acquittal'; and we have evidence of this other than that of
an enthusiast, in the fact that their contempt of death was actually one
of the charges brought against the Christians by the heathen. 'Unhappy
men!' exclaimed the proconsul Arrius Antoninus on seeing all the Christians of a certain town in Asia present themselves at his bar, though
they know well the consequencs; 'if you are weary of your lives, cannot
you find halters and precipices?' 'Go, then, and kill yourselves,' cried
another in derision, 'and pass to your God, but do not trouble us.' 'As a
rule,' said the Emperor Diocletian, 'the Christians are only too happy to
die' – and Diocletian certainly was in a position to know. Eusebius, an
eye-witness, tells us that the martyrs of the Thebais, in the time of
Diocletian, 'received the sentence of death with gladness and exultation,
so far even as to sing hymns of praise and thanksgiving until they
breathed their last.' For they believed that after death the—

angels would carry them eastward, past the storehouse of hail and snow,
past the fountains of rain, past the spirits of wickedness which are in the

air, and carry them to the seventh circle, setting them down full opposite the glory of God.

'Why are you so bent upon death?' said an official to the martyr Pionius of Smyrna. 'You are so bent upon death,' he added, 'that you make nothing of it.' 'We are bent, not upon death,' replied Pionius, 'but upon life.' When nailed to the cross, the officer made one last effort to induce him to recant. 'Carry out the edict,' he promised, 'and the nails shall be withdrawn.' 'I felt that they were in,' was the answer, as, turning to the people, he bid them remember that 'after death came the resurrection.' When the fires were lighted, 'with joyous countenance, he cried, Amen', 'So he too,' adds the chronicler, 'passed through the narrow gate to the large place and great light.' 'Will you be with us, or with your Christ?' asked the governor, as they hung Nestor, bishop of Perga, the chief city of Pamphylia, 'well strapped and curry-combed,' upon the cross. The bishop answered: 'With Christ I am, and always was, and always shall be'. When Nicander, a soldier quartered in Moesia (Bulgaria), arrived at the place of execution, his wife Daria was brought to his side. 'God be with you,' said the husband. 'Be of good cheer,' replied the wife, for whom the years of separation when she was a Christian and he a heathen still were now at an end—

play the hero. Ten years I spent at home without you, and every moment I prayed God that I might see you. Now I have seen you, I rejoice that you are setting out for life. How loud shall I sing, and how proud I am that soon I shall be a martyr's wife! So be of good cheer, and bear your witness to God.

When Irenaeus of Sirmium was condemned to be thrown into the Save, his face showed his disappointment—

'I expected,' he said, 'many tortures. Torture me, I beseech you, that you may learn how Christians, because of their faith in God, have schooled themselves to despise death.'

Of Victor, the father of the martyr Maximilian of Theveste, we read that after the execution—

he returned to the house with great joy, thanking God that he had sent on such a gift before him, and determined to follow after.

In no document of the early church is the ecstasy of the martyrs, and their indifference to – we might almost call it their enthusiasm for – death more clearly brought out than in the *Epistles of Ignatius*, though no doubt some allowance must be made for the excitable Syrian nature. Of the circumstances which led to the condemnation of Ignatius, the second bishop of Antioch and metropolitan of Syria, we know nothing. The persecution at Antioch, by no means limited to Ignatius, has left no other memorials of itself than these *Epistles*. As a rule Christians, unless Roman citizens, were executed in the place of their crime; but for special reasons, probably connected with the extraordinary spectacles which Trajan had given in the Coliseum, whose magnitude had long since drained Rome of both gladiators and criminals, Theophorus Ignatius 'entwined with saintly fetters, the diadem of the truly elect', was sent from Antioch to Rome, 'to make a Roman holiday'. He tells us that he was in the charge of ten soldiers, whom he compares, with a touch of humour, to 'ten leopards'. Every effort on the part of himself and his friends to appease them only led to fresh cruelties in the hope, probably, of fresh exactions. The details of this journey of Ignatius, the letters which he wrote *en route* to various churches, with their wealth of intercourse and love, need not concern us. At Smyrna he held delightful fellowship with one destined in later years to tread the narrow way himself, the bishop Polycarp. Landing in Europe in the footsteps of St. Paul, we lose sight of him after Philippi. The rest is only legend. But there is little doubt that, as Origen tells us, in a fight with wild beasts, in the Coliseum at Rome, Ignatius, whom Lightfoot well calls 'the captain of martyrs,' paid the price of his faith with his own life about the same time as his fellow-Christians in Bithynia suffered under Pliny and Trajan.

In his *Epistle to the Romans* – 'his paean prophetic of the coming victory' – Ignatius had already anticipated the final act in his description of himself as 'God's wheat, ground fine by the teeth of wild beasts, that he may be found pure bread, a sacrifice to God'. In more than one passage we see Ignatius not so much resigned as eager for the day of martyrdom – 'in the midst of life, yet lusting after death.' He realizes all the struggle, he is more than assured of the victory:

Come fire, and cross, and grapplings with wild beasts, cuttings and manglings, wrenchings of bones, breaking of limbs, crushing of my whole body, come cruel tortures of the devil to assail me. Only be it mine to attain unto Jesus Christ.

In passages such as these we hear the shout of one triumphant already, who felt 'the pangs of the new birth' upon him. 'Near the sword,' he cries, 'the nearer to God; in company with wild beasts, in company with God.' 'Do not hinder me,' he continues – he refers to some possible appeal by influential parties at Rome to the emperor, which might save him—

from living, do not desire my death. . . . Suffer me to receive the pure light.

When I am come to the arena, then shall I become a man. Permit me to be an imitator of the passion of my God.

He bids men 'sing a chorus of love to the Father' for the grace that is his, 'to be poured out as a libation to God.' For he is assured: 'If I shall suffer, then am I a freed man of Jesus Christ, and I shall rise free in Him'. So he prays that he

may have joy in the beasts, and find them prompt. If not I will entice them that they may devour me promptly, not as they have done to some, refusing to touch them through fear (*Rom.* 5).

V

Many there were, among them not a few clerics, whom the hour of trial found wanting, who in the expressive phrase of Ignatius 'hawked about the Name'. For there is nothing which so tests the reality of faith as the call to the great renunciation. Nor must we overlook how easy recantation designedly had been made. For, as Tertullian pointed out, there was this curious feature about Christianity, distinguishing it from every other criminal charge, that a mere denial was sufficient to procure acquittal. There were degrees and stages of apostasy. Some, who had no deepness of root, 'when the sun was risen, withered away'. As the Christians of Lyons wrote with sadness of ten of their number, 'they were unable to bear the tension of a great conflict.' 'Many of our brethren,' adds Cyprian—

vanquished before the fight, did not even make a show of sacrificing under compulsion. They ran of their own account to the Forum, as if they were indulging a long-cherished desire. There you could see them entreating the magistrates to receive their recantations, although it was already night (*de Lapsis* 8).

Such apostates, when brought before the altar, 'stood pale and trembling, as if they were not to sacrifice, but themselves to be the sacrifice'. A few, not content with denying their Lord, under the terror of pain betrayed their brethren. Some there were, of stouter faith, who could endure days of imprisonment, but whom torture or the horrid anticipation thereof overcame. Nor were those who had thrust themselves forward for martyrdom always the most courageous. At the supreme moment their enthusiasm failed, and they denied the faith for which the Much-afraids unhesitatingly laid down their lives. We have an instance of this in the case of Quintus the Phrygian, at the time of the martyrdom of Polycarp. (*Mart. Polyc.*4.)

Others again, who did not actually recant, did not scruple to purchase the necessary certificates of sacrifice (*libelli*) from easy-going magistrates, or to use those procured for them by anxious pagan friends. We hear also of some Christians of the baser sort who sent their Christian slaves to represent them at the sacrifice, or who succeeded in bribing the attendants to let them slip past the altar without actual sacrifice or eating of the sacrifices. These certificates, which form such a feature in the persecution of Decius, were probably all of similar form, and ran as follows (we quote from one discovered in the Fayûm in 1893, and now at Berlin):

To the Commissioners of sacrifice of the village of Alexander's Island, from Aurelius Diogenes, the son of Satabus, of the village of Alexander's Island, aged 72; scar on his right eyebrow
I have always sacrificed regularly to the gods, and now, in your presence, in accordance with the edict, I have done sacrifice, and poured the drink-offering, and tasted of the sacrifices, and I request you to certify the same. Farewell.

> Handed in by me, *Aurelius Diogenes.*
> I certify that I saw Him Sacrificing, ... *nonus.*
> (Magistrate's signature partly obliterated.)

In the first year of the Emperor, Caesar Gaius Messius Quintus Trajanus Decius, Pius, Felix, Augustus; the second of the month Epith.

For others, true saints of god, there were, as for Simon Peter, moments of weakness over which they wept bitter tears. One woman tore with her teeth the tongue which had denied her Lord. Some, of whom the *Shepherd* Hermas tells us, 'became cowards, and were lost in uncertainty, and considered in their hearts whether they should deny or confess, and yet finally suffered' for the faith. Of such was a woman at Lyons, Biblias, who at first denied, but when brought out by the authorities to bear witness of atheism against her fellow Christians, 'awoke, as it were, out of a deep sleep, and was added to the number of the martyrs'.

Of cases of recantation, one of the most interesting will be found in the records of the martyrdom of Pionius and his comrades. Not the least of the tortures of that brave band of Christians lay in the knowledge that their bishop, Euctemon, had fallen away like Judas. Pionius and others were dragged to the temple at the instigation, it was said, of Euctemon himself, in the hope that the example of their superior might lead to their own fall. On arrival they flung themselves to the ground, but six constables held Pionius fast and brought him to the altar, struggling and shouting, 'We are Christians'. There the apostate bishop, with garland on his forehead, was still standing beside his sacrifice, part of which he had reserved to take home in order that he might hold a feast. But backsliders, so hardened in their crime, were not common.

VI

We must bring this study of persecution to a close. But there are one or two deductions which may be gathered on which a word is advisable.

In the Church, as in the world, the wheat and the tares grow together; the image of gold is always mixed with clay. So it has proved in the case of the martyrs. The danger of all forms of self-renunciation is the mistaking the means as an end in itself. We see examples of this in Monasticism and Puritanism; and the same thing happened in the early Church. At times there swept over all sections an extravagant thirst for self-immolation, and Christians, in plain disregard of the teaching of Jesus, courted death with culpable recklessness, and exalted martyrdom into the one royal road to perfection.

'What did they suffer?' says I. 'Listen,' saith she. 'Stripes, imprisonments, great tribulations, crosses, wild beasts, for the Name's sake. Therefore to them belongs the right side of the holiness of God, to them and to all who shall suffer for the Name. But for the rest is the left side' (Herm. *Shep.* Vis. iii 2).

By martyrdom—

> the frail becomes the perfect, rapt
> From glory of pain to glory of joy.

'Let me be given to the wild beasts,' cries Ignatius, 'for through them I can attain unto God.' By martyrdom 'all sins were healed'. Persecution was the 'second baptism in blood which stands in lieu of fontal baptism when that has not been received, and restores it when lost.' A certificate from a martyr, transferring, so to speak, his merit to another, not always specifically named, was looked upon by the lapsed as sufficient pardon for their denial of their Lord, a door of repentance, as Cyprian complained, 'very wide indeed,' a cause of much trouble to the early Church, especially in North Africa, and which led in later times to further erroneous developments of the doctrine of Indulgences.

Materialism, in one or other of its many forms, is ever the great enemy against which the spiritual has to fight; and of all forms of materialism the most dangerous, because the most insidious, is that which entrenches itself within the Church itself. Unfortunately nothing more assisted the growing materialism in spiritual life in its worst forms than the excessive regard felt by the Church for her martyrs. When Gregory Thaumaturgus began the system of substituting for pagan feasts wakes over the remains of martyrs, he struck a blow, unconscious but profound, as we may see from the later mediaeval corruptions, at spiritual life itself. From this to the vast system of the veneration of relics for their own sakes, and the attributing to them every conceivable form of miraculous power, was but a step, the disasters of which are writ large in the whole history of the Church. The apotheosis against which the martyrs had protested in the case of the emperors, was now introduced into the Church in the guise of semi-divine apostles and saints. Even Lucian had noted the danger, as we see from his sneer that after his death Peregrinus passed as a god among the Christians.

But to dwell on these things is an ungrateful task. Rather let us turn to the wreath of gold which the martyrs laid at the feet of the crucified Christ. Purposeless renunciation, the renunciation of dervish or fakir, can never appeal to the Western world. But the renunciation of the martyrs was neither purposeless nor self-centred. As their name shows, they were 'witnesses'; as the needle turns to the Pole, so they must point, not to themselves, but to another. Every martyr's death was an emphatic *credo*, uttered in a language that all could understand.

'See Socrates,' exclaims Justin Martyr, 'no one trusted in him so as to die for his doctrine: but in Christ . . . not only philosophers and scholars believed, but also artisans, and people illiterate' (II *Apol.* 10).

They made this manifest by 'despising both glory and fear and death'. We may own with Tertullian that the argument, historically considered, is not perfectly sound. But in reality it fitted in not merely with the experience of Justin Martyr himself, but with that of thousands of others.

For I myself, when I was contented with the doctrines of Plato, and heard the Christians slandered, yet saw them fearless of death and of everything that men count terrible, felt that it was impossible that these men could be living, as was reputed, in wickedness and mere pleasure (II *Apol.* 12).

We see this power of conviction of which Justin speaks in the records, too numerous to be later inventions, of those who were won to Christ by witnessing the martyr's death, or by having the custody of the prisoners in their last hours. One illustration may suffice – that of a young officer of the court in attendance on Galerius, who was so impressed by the faith of the confessors at Nicomedeia that he asked them the secret of their courage, and, on receiving instruction, when next the Christians were examined, stepped forward and requested Galerius to make a note of his name among theirs. 'Are you mad?' asked Galerius. 'Do you wish to throw away your life?' 'I am not mad,' was the reply. 'I was mad once, but am now in my right mind.' After many tortures he won his crown. In his case, as in countless conversions in every age, it was not full-orbed knowledge of Christian truth, but one ray of light that wrought the change. The confession 'Jesus is Lord' was sufficient.

The martyrs also were witnesses to a creed, simple it is true, but none the less definite and real. They did not lay down their lives for vague generalities, wider visions, or larger hopes. They knew not only in whom, but in what they believed, and bore witness before judge and mob, oftentimes with their dying breath, to the vitalizing power of a concrete and definite faith. In the later stories of the martyrs there is a tendency to amplify their creeds, to turn them from their simplicity into argumentative and theological systems. In the earlier records, however, faith is not a philosophy, but dwells rather on the central truths which to the martyr seemed so all-important that for them he would lay down life itself. Prominent among these was the belief in his own immortality as the result of the resurrection of his Lord. But the central 'witness' of the martyrs was to the living reality of the person of Christ, and to 'the reign of the Eternal King'. In bearing this testimony they shared the power of such beliefs to exalt human nature. By his death the martyr proved that man 'was more than a dull jest'. An instance will illustrate our meaning. Let the reader contrast the typical slave as depicted in the pages of Plautus or Terence with the slave that we see, not once nor twice, ennobling the annals of the Church. The slave of Terence may be exceptional – in his wit he certainly was – and so also was the slave-martyr. But this does not alter our argument, the contrast of the ideals they represent. In the records of slave-martyrs we have the witness to a social revolution going on in the world, the depth and meaning of which was probably hidden even from the Christians themselves. 'And you too, Evelpistus, what are you?' said the judge Rusticus, the friend of Marcus Aurelius, to one of the companions of Justin, a slave in Caesar's household. 'I am a Christian,' was the reply, 'set free by Christ.'

Nowhere do we see this more beautifully brought out than in the case of Blandina, the slave-girl of Lyons. Even her mistress had feared for her 'that she would not be able to make a bold confession on account of the weakness of her body'. But after the tormentors had tortured her 'from morning until evening, until they were tired and weary, confessing that they were baffled, for they had no other tortures that they could apply to her', her fellow-Christians realized that 'in Blandina Christ showed that the things which to man appear mean and deformed and contemptible are with God deemed worthy of great honour'. So when finally she was

hung up, fastened to a stake in the shape of a cross, as food for the wild beasts that were let loose against her, she inspired the others with great eagerness, for in the combat of their sister they saw Him who was crucified for them. . . . And after she had been scourged, and exposed to the wild beasts, and roasted in the iron chair, she was at last enclosed in a net and cast before a bull.

So Blandina passed over 'as one invited to a marriage supper', and sat down with Vettius Epagathus, the rich young nobleman, in the King's presence.

The consideration of the triumph of Blandina, and of the hundreds of others of whom she is but a representative, leads us to ask a question? We do so in the words of a great master of English:

> Whence came this tremendous spirit, scaring, nay offending, the criticism of our delicate days? Does Gibbon think to sound the depths of eternal ocean with the tape and measuring-rod of merely literary philosophy?

We would quote in answer the wise summary of a recent secular historian, whose study of the principate of Nero has led him to survey the conflict and its issue:

> We may not under-rate the 'secondary causes' of Christianity's growth. But neither may we neglect the external circumstances which promised only, it might seem, too surely to destroy it altogether. Persecution may be a sign of strength. It is hardly a cause of strength when it is cruel and persistent. . . . Persecution may kill a religion and destroy it utterly, if that religion's strength lies only in its numbers, by a simple process of exhaustion. The opinion that no belief, no moral conviction, can be eradicated from a country by persecution is a grave popular fallacy.

Christianity, we conclude, answered man's needs and his cry for aid, articulate and inarticulate, conscious or unconscious, in the early days of the Roman Empire, as did no other creed or philosophy. When, however, we face soberly the questions whence came such a creed into existence which could satisfy human wants, as none other before or since, and how came the new, despised, and persecuted religion to overcome perils and dangers of a terrible kind, with no external agency in its favour and every external power ranged against it, we do not feel inclined to deduce the rapidity of its growth and its victory over all opponents from a mere balance of its internal advantages over its external disqualifications. We admit the vigorous secondary causes of its growth, but we have left its origin unexplained, and cannot but see as well the vigour and strength of the foes which willed its destruction and powerfully dissuaded from its acceptance. And there exists for us, as historians, no secondary nor human cause or combination of causes sufficient to account for the triumph of Christianity.

There is but one sufficient explanation: the new religion descended 'out of heaven from God'.

We have pointed out already that the martyrs were witnesses to the absoluteness of the Christian faith, that the religion of Jesus would have nothing to do with the current syncretism. Time after time we find judges, either actuated by mercy or prompted by their 'philosophy', striving to draw the martyrs into syncretistic admissions which would have given them their liberty. But the martyrs refused to purchase life by any compromise between their faith and 'the world'. Well would it be for the Church today if she could learn the lesson they taught. The fashionable syncretism of the empire has passed away; men are no longer intent on the identification of the gods of Greece and Rome. In its place we see a more dangerous fusion, the identification of the world and the Church, the syncretism of material and spiritual things. We need once more to catch the martyr-spirit, a belief in the absoluteness of the Christian faith translated into facts which shall make the Church 'a peculiar people', whose strength does not lie in any blending of light and darkness, but in her renunciation of and aloofness from 'the world'.

The resolute renunciation of the world, of which the martyrs were the crown and symbol, did more than anything else to make the Church strong to conquer the world. The martyrs were witnesses to the truth that only by renouncing the world can we really do anything for it. Critics of different schools have found fault with primitive Christianity for being too unworldly and ascetic, and have pointed to the more excellent means of modern times. But twentieth-century ideals of renunciation would never have effected the gigantic revolution which sapped and dissolved gigantic polytheisms, and overthrew the Roman Empire itself. *Vicisti Galilaee* is not merely the selfconscious cry of a dying paganism; it is the splendid testimony wrung from reluctant lips to the power of the ideals of the Cross.

For the obedience unto death of those who followed the Lamb whithersoever He went, partook also of the persuasiveness of the supreme Sacrifice. In the noble army of martyrs we salute the conquerors of the world. In the fine figure of Justin the Church was a vine which, the more it bled under the pruning-knife, the more fruitful it became. 'The more men multiply our sufferings, the more does the number of the faithful grow.' For in the words of the dying martyrs men heard the voice of the Holy Spirit, 'convicting the world of sin, of righteousness, and of judgement'. The proud boast of Tertullian was correct. 'The blood of the martyrs is indeed the seed of the Church. Dying we conquer. The moment we are crushed, that moment we go forth victorious.'

SELECT BIBLIOGRAPHY

A. SOURCES

English translations of the main documents will be found in the following books:

The Acts of the Christian Martyrs, texts and translation by Herbert Musurillo, Oxford Early Christian Texts, ed. H. Chadwick (OUP, 1972). (Not without faults; see Professor Fergus Millar's review in *Journal of Theological Studies* (=JTS) NS xxiv 1973, 239–243, but text and translation are arranged side by side and there are useful bibliographical notes.)

E.C.E. Owen, *Some Authentic Acts of the Early Martyrs*, (Oxford, 1927). (Still a useful stand-by, as also is the selection, *Ausgewählte Martyrerakten*, ed. R. Knopf and G. Krüger, Mohr, Tübingen, 1929.)

J. Stevenson, *A New Eusebius* (SPCK, London, 1957). (Contains some of the key documents not in the above title.)

See in particular, also, G. Lanata, *Gli atti dei martiri come documenti processuali* (Giuffre, Milan, 1973). (A fine study without English translation but including excellent bibliographical notes and critical evaluation of manuscript traditions.)

B. CURRENT LITERATURE

Since Workman's day, the balance of research has changed from the establishment of the facts about the persecutions to an understanding of the position of the Christians in Greco-Roman provincial society. The aspects of 'opposition cult' and 'illegal society', the latter stressed by Celsus (Origen, *Contra Celsum* 1.1) have invited investigation and debate, and Celsus himself emerges as the most important witness to the character of Christianity in the second century. For the third century the persecutions are to be seen against the background of the continuous expansion of Christianity and its survival in face of the decay of many forms of traditional religious life during the disasters of the period.

The best modern short account of the persecutions is by G.E.M. de Ste. Croix, 'Why were the early Christians persecuted?', *Past and Present* (=PP) 26 Nov. 1963, 6–38, and reproduced in *Studies in Ancient History*, ed. M. I. Finley (RKP, London, 1974), 210–250.

A fuller account will be found in W. H. C. Frend, *Martyrdom and Persecution in the Early Church* (Blackwell's, Oxford, 1965). (Bibliography to 1964.)

For classic statements, still valuable, see:

E. G. Hardy, *Christianity and the Roman Government* (London, 1894, reprinted 1925).

N. H. Baynes, 'The Great Persecution', ch.xix of *Cambridge Ancient History*, vol. xii (CUP, 1939).

Useful studies on particular issues are:

T. D. Barnes, 'Legislation against the Christians', *Journal of Roman Studies*, lviii, 1968, 32–50, and 'Pre-Decian *Acta Martyrorum*', JTS, NS xix, 1968, 509–531.

E. J. Bickerman, 'Trajan, Hadrian and the Christians', *Rivista di Filologia e di istruzione classica* (Turin) 96, 1968, 3, 290–315.

G. W. Clarke, 'Some Observations on the Persecution of Decius', *Antichthon* (Sydney University Press, 1969) iii, 63–76.

W. H. C. Frend, 'The Persecutions: Links between Judaism and the Early Church', *Journal of Ecclesiastical History* (=JEH), ix 2, 1958, 141–158, and 'The Gnostic Sects and the Roman Empire', JEH, v 1, 1954, 25–37.

H. Grégoire, 'Les Persécutions dans l'Empire Romain', *Mémoires de L'Academie royale de Belgique* xlvi l, 1951.

Paul Keretzes, 'The Peace of Gallienus', *Wiener Studien*, N. F. 9, 1975, 174–185, and 'Marcus Aurelius a Persecutor?', *Harvard Theological Review* (=HTR), 61, 3, 1968, 321–341.

J. H. Knipfing, 'The *Libelli* of the Decian Persecution', HTR, 16, 1923, 345–390.

J. Molthagen, *Der römische Staat und die Christen im zweiten und dritten Jahrhundert* (Göttingen, 1970).

J. Moreau, *La Persécution du Christianisme dans l'Empire Romain*, (Paris, 1956) (revised German ed. Saarbrücken, 1961).

G. E. M. de Ste. Croix, 'Aspects of the "Great" Persecution', HTR, 47, 1954, 75–113.

M. Sordi, *Il Cristianesimo e Roma*, T. Cappelli (Bologna, 1965).

J. Stevenson, *The Catacombs* (Thames and Hudson, London, 1978).

J. Vogt, 'Zur Religiosität der Christenverfolger im römischen Reich', *Sitzungsberichter Akademie Heidelberger*, Phil. Hist. KL 1962, and with H. Last, 'Christenverfolgungen', i Historisch (Vogt), ii Juristisch (Last), in *Reallexikon für Antike und Christentum* ii, 1954, 1159ff.

A. N. Sherwin-White, 'The Early Persecutions and Roman Law Again', JTS, NS iii, 1952, 199–213, and his discussion with Ste. Croix in 'An Amendment' PP (April, 1964), 23–27 and Ste. Croix's reply 'A rejoinder', ibid. 28–33. Also, edited by Sherwin-White, *The Letters of Pliny* (OUP, 1966), 691–712. (A detailed discussion of the Pliny-Trajan correspondence.)

A. Wlosok, *Rom und die Christen*, Klett (Stuttgart, 1970).

W. H. C. Frend
September 1979

CHRONOLOGICAL TABLE

revised by Professor W. H. C. Frend

General History	Christians and the Roman Empire
April 30 (?). Crucifixion of Jesus.	
16 Mar. 37. Death of Tiberius.	
18 Mar. 37–24 Jan. 41. CAIUS (Caligula) emperor.	41–44. Agrippa I king of Judaea, Samaria and Northern Palestine. Martyrdom of James (Zebedee).
	49 (?). Banishment of Jews from Rome.
Oct. 54–9 June 68. NERO emperor.	58. Arrest of Paul at Jerusalem.
	59. Procurator Festus sends Paul to Rome, where he arrives circa Mar. 60.
	62. Judicial murder of James the Just in Jerusalem.
19 July 64. Burning of Rome.	64. Arrest and persecution of the Christians (martyrdom of Peter?).
66–73. Jewish Revolt in Palestine.	
68–69. Year of the Four Emperors.	
1 July 69–23 June 79. VESPASIAN emperor.	
August 70. Titus takes Jerusalem. Destruction of the Temple.	70. Part of the *Apocalypse* written (?).
23 June 79–13 Sept. 81. TITUS emperor.	
13 Sept. 81–18 Sept. 96. DOMITIAN emperor.	95. Domitian acts against high-born Jewish proselytes and Christians (?). Execution of Acilius Glabrio. Exile of Flavia Domitilla to Pandetaria.
	96. Publication of the *Apoclypse* in present form (?). Recall of those exiled by Domitian.
Sept. 96–27 Jan. 98. NERVA emperor.	97. (?). *First Epistle of Clement* written.
27 Jan. 98–Aug. 117. TRAJAN emperor.	104 (?). Martyrdom of Symeon, Bishop of Jerusalem.

General History	Christians and the Roman Empire
	107/8. Martyrdom of Ignatius of Antioch (*Letters* of Ignatius).
	112–113. Pliny–Trajan correspondence concerning the Christians.
115–117. *Annals* of Tacitus written.	
11 Aug. 117–July 138. HADRIAN emperor.	
120. Suetonius' *De Vitis Caesarum*.	
128–29. Hadrian's Wall.	124–125. Hadrian's Rescript to Minucius Fundanus, Proconsul of Asia.
130. Aelia Capitolina founded.	130–180. Gnostic teachers in Alexandria.
	c. 130. Conversion of Justin Martyr.
132–135. Bar-Kokba war. (Persecution of Christians by the Palestinian Jews).	*c.* 137. Martyrdom of Telesphorus, Bishop of Rome.
10 July 138–7 Mar. 161. ANTONINUS PIUS emperor.	
142. Antonine Wall between Forth and Clyde.	144. Marcion's schism.
	c. 145. Apology of Aristides.
	c. 150. Rescripts to the Assembly of the province of Achaea, and cities of Athens, Larissa and Thessalonica.
	150. Justin's *First Apology*.
	23 Feb. 156 (or 165). Martyrdom of Polycarp of Smyrna.
	157 (or 172). Beginnings of Montanism in Phyrgia.
	c. 160. Peregrinus (pseudo-confessor).
7 Mar. 161–17 Mar. 180. MARCUS AURELIUS emperor.	*c.* 162. Ptolemy and Lucius martyred at Rome. Justin's *Second Apology*.
161–166. Parthian War.	165. Justin martyred at Rome.
	165. Peregrinus immolates himself at Olympiad Games.
	165 (?). Rescript of the Proconsul of Asia (?) unfavourable to Christians.
	167 (?). Martyrdom of Sagaris, Thraseas and others in Asia.
166–180. Wars against barbarians on the Danube (episode of the 'Thundering Legion').	169–180. Spate of Christian Apologies.
176. COMMODUS joint emperor.	*c.* 176. Melito of Sardis writes.

General History	Christians and the Roman Empire
	177. Athenagoras' *Plea*.
	177. Martyrdoms at Lyons. Rescript to provincial governor from emperor.
c. 178. Marcus Aurelius' *Meditations*.	*c. 178.* Celsus writes *The True Word* against the Christians.
17 *Mar.* 180–31 *Dec.* 192. COMMODUS *emperor*.	*c.* 180. Theophilus of Antioch writes *Ad Autolycum*.
	July 180. Martyrs of Scilii.
	180–185 (?). Martyrdom of Apollonius at Rome.
	185–192. Marcia's influence with Commodus in favour of Christians.
	185. Birth of Origen.
	c. 185. Irenaeus writes *Against the Heresies*.
	185 (?). Further martyrdoms in Asia under Proconsul Arrius Antoninus.
31 *Dec.* 192. Murder of Commodus.	*c.* 190. First evidence of Christian property-holding in Rome. The community's catacomb administered by the deacon Callistus.
13 *Apr.* 193. SEPTIMIUS SEVERIUS proclaimed emperor.	
193–197. Civil wars in the empire, from which Septimius Severus emerges victorious.	*c.* 195. Clement of Alexandria compiles the *Stromateis*.
197–235. Exaltation of Imperial Cult under the Severan dynasty.	197. Tertullian's *Apology*.
	202–206. Severe but sporadic outbreaks directed principally against Christian converts (Martyrdom of Perpetua and companions at Carthage 7 Mar. 203, and Origen's father Leonides in Alexandria).
	c. 207. Tertullian joins the Montanists.
4 *Feb.* 211. Severus dies at York after three-year campaign against tribes in Scotland. CARACALLA and GETA emperors.	211–212. Tertullian writes his *De Fuga* and *De Corona Militari*.
27 *Feb.* 212. Geta murdered. Caracalla sole emperor.	212/13. Tertullian writes *Ad Scapulam* after local persecution.
c. 215. Philostratus writes his *Life of Apollonius* of Tyana.	214. Origen visits provincial governor of Arabia.

218– Mar. 222. ELAGABALUS emperor.

218–222. Callistus Bishop of Rome. Tertullian writes *De Pudicitia*.

10 Mar. 222–22 Mar. 235. ALEXANDER SEVERUS emperor.

213–235. Period of toleration for Christians. Building of Christian house-church at Dura Europos in c. 230.

224. Sassanian revolution in Parthia.

234. Attacks by Alemanni on Rhine frontier.

232. Origen meets the empress Julia Mammaea at Antioch.

235. Murder of Alexander Severus at Mainz. His supplanter MAXIMIN THRAX accepted as emperor by the Senate.

235. Anti-Christian measures directed principally against the leadership of the Church. Bishop Pontian and Hippolytus exiled. Origen writes his *Exhortation to Martyrdom*.

238. Revolt in North Africa. Overthrow of Maximin.

Apr. 240. Mani begins to preach his new religion.

9 July 238. GORDIAN III proclaimed emperor.

Mar. 244. Murder of Gordian. PHILIP THE ARABIAN recognized as emperor.

c. 243. Beginning of Gregory the Wonderworker's mission in Pontus.

c. 245. Conversion of Cyprian of Carthage.

247. Celebration of the 1000th anniversary of the founding of Rome.

247–264. Dionysius Bishop of Alexandria.

248. Goths attack Danube frontier.

248. Origen writes *Contra Celsum*.

Dec. 248–June 251. DECIUS emperor.

248. Cyprian elected Bishop of Carthage.

248. Anti-Christian *pogrom* in Alexandria.

Jan. 250. Arrest and execution of Christian leaders. Fabian, Bishop of Rome, martyred 20 Jan. 250.

June 251. Decius killed in battle against the Goths.

Spring/Summer 250. General sacrifice ordered throughout empire. Persecution of Christians. Cyprian in hiding. Egyptian *libelli*, June–July.

Aug. 251–May 253. GALLUS emperor.

251. Cyprian writes *De Lapsis* and *De Unitate ecclesiae catholicae*.

Oct. 253–June 260. VALERIAN emperor.

252. Threat of renewed persecution.

254–56. Persian war. Fall of Dura Europos and Nisibis to the Persians.

254–256. Church Councils held in Carthage.

Aug. 257. First Rescript of Valerian against the Christians. Dionysius of Alexandria and Cyprian exiled.

General History	Christians and the Roman Empire
259. Renewal of Persian War. *June* 260. Valerian captured by Persians near Edessa. 260–268. GALLIENUS emperor. *July* 260. End of persecution. Barbarian pressure on Rhine and Danube frontiers continues. 268–270. CLAUDIUS II emperor. Goths decisively defeated at Naissus (Nish).	*July* 258. Second Rescript against the Christians. Pope Xystus and deacons martyred 6 Aug. Cyprian martyred, 14 Sep. 258. 262. Paul of Samosata Bishop of Antioch. Acts as financial administrator (*duenarius*) to Queen Zenobia of Palmyra. 264, 265, 268. Councils directed against Paul. 272. Appeal by Church of Antioch to Aurelian against Paul. Aurelian's decision leads to Paul's deposition. 275. Threat of persecution against the Christians.
17 *Sep.* 284–1 *May* 305. DIOCLETIAN emperor. *Mar.* 286. MAXIMIAN associated with Diocletian. 1 *Mar.* 293. Association of the two Caesars, Constantius and Galerius. Diocletian reforms Army, provincial administration and currency. 297–298. Persian war. Galerius victorious. 301. Edict of Prices. 20 *Nov.* 303. Diocletian celebrates *Vicennalia* at Rome. 304. Diocletian's illness. Galcrius takes over control of eastern part of empire. 1 *May* 305. Diocletian and Maximian abdicate. Constantius and Galerius *Augusti*, Maximian and Severus, *Caesars*. 25 *July* 306. Death of Constantius at York. Constantine declared Augustus by his father's troops. 26 *Oct.* 306. MAXENTIUS, son of Maximian declared emperor (*princeps*) at Rome. 11 *Nov.* 308. Licinius elevated to the rank of Augustus. (Conference of Carnuntum)	298. Christians dismissed from imperial service. 23 *Feb.* 303. Great Persecution begins. Christian buildings to be destroyed and sacred books to be handed over. *Summer* 303. Bishops imprisoned (and forced to participate in sacrifices). *Spring* 304. The Fourth Edict of Persecution. General sacrifice ordered. 306–310. Continuance of persecution in the east by Galerius and Maximin. Death of Pamphilus.

General History	Christians and the Roman Empire
310. Constantine rids himself of Maximian. 'Pagan vision' of Constantine.	310–312. Maximin attempts to reform pagan cult.
311. Galerius' illness. Dies 5 May.	30 *April* 311. Galerius' Edict of Toleration.
	311–312. Covert acts of persecution in the east. Martyrdom of Peter of Alexandria, 25 Nov. 311, and Lucian of Antioch, 7 Jan. 312.
	311. Eusebius ends first eight books of the *Ecclesiastical History*.
312. Constantine invades Italy.	312. Outbreak of Donatist Controversy.
28 *Oct.* 312. Constantine defeats and slays Maxentius at the Battle of the Mulvian Bridge.	
Feb. 313. Meets Licinius at Milan.	313. Edict of Milan ends the Great Persecution.
30 *April* 313. Maximin defeated by Licinius near Adrianople (dies summer 313).	
314 (or 316). War between Constantine and Licinius.	314–16. Lactantius writes his *Institutes* and *On the Deaths of the Persecutors*.
	Aug. 314. Council of Arles.
	314–321. Constantine increasingly favours the Christians by legislation, donations and conferment of immunities.
316. Constantine decides against the Donatists.	315. Lactantius appointed tutor to his son, Crispus.
	318. Outbreak of Arian controversy in Alexandria.
	322. Beginning of the building of St. Peter's at Rome.
324. Second war against Licinius. CONSTANTINE victorious at Battle of Chrysopolis (18 Sep.). Sole emperor.	322–324. Licinius' vexatious acts against the Christians.
	Oct. 324. Constantine proclaims Christianity as the religion of the empire.
	324–325. Eusebius issues final edition of his *Ecclesiastical History*.
	20 *May* 325. Meeting of the Council of Nicaea.